For Nikki!
Michelle Dunn

How to Make Money Collecting Money, Starting a Collection Agency, Third Edition

Third Edition

Never Dunn Publishing LLC • Plymouth, New Hampshire

By Michelle Dunn
©2008 Michelle Dunn

Published by:

Never Dunn Publishing LLC
PO Box 40
Plymouth NH 03264

www.michelledunn.com
www.credit-and-collections.com

Cover design, book layout, and production by
WoW! Graphic Designs www.wowgraphicdesigns.com • 800-962-4254

Author photos by Timothy Cameron, Achber Studio, Laconia, NH

Editing by provided by Arlene Stoppe

ISBN 978-0-9706645-6-3

55795

9 780970 664563

Library of Congress control Number: TX 6-205-251

This book is designed to provide accurate and authoritative information in regard to the subject matter covered. It is sold with the understanding that the author is not engaged in rendering legal advice or services. If legal advice is required, please see your attorney.

Printed in the United States of America.

Never Dunn

Publishing

Disclaimer

This book is designed to provide information to help you start up and run your own debt collection agency. It is sold with the understanding that the publisher and author are not giving legal, accounting or other professional advice or services. The content of this book is based on my own personal research and experience. If legal or other assistance is required, please see your attorney or accountant.

Every effort has been made to make this book as accurate as possible. However, there may be mistakes. This book is sold as a guide with what information is current as of the date of the original printing.

This book is sold to provide information and guidance. Never Dunn Publishing LLC, and Michelle Dunn shall have no liability or responsibility to any person or entity for any damage or alleged damage caused directly or indirectly by the information contained in this book.

Imagine what happens when you start your own collection agency and when your mail is delivered all you receive is checks!

What people are saying about this book:

"Dunn's self published title, How to Make Money Collecting Money, Starting a Collection Agency, is a very well laid out book in both design and content," says Writer's Digest. "The text is logical and easy to follow. The samples are effective and easily understood. The flow between chapters makes it easy to follow. A good cover and a good job of selling the book on the back cover also lead to its success." –**Writer's Digest**

"Michelle Dunn has helped to bring the collection industry to a more reputable light. Collection Agencies have taken a bad rap in the past and she has helped to dignify our industry with her integrity and knowledge. Her books are well thought out, her website is helpful and her e-mail group serves as a wealth of knowledge to our industry." –**Jan Conte, President, Your Collection Solution, LLC**

"I asked Michelle Dunn to take part in a diary book project called 'This Day' because I wanted to find out what the life of a collection agent was really like (How do you track down someone who owes you money when they won't answer their phone? How do you tell a burly guy who defaulted on his car loan that you're going to take his car?). Michelle's book, Starting a Collection Agency takes a day in the life a step further by showing you how to actually get started as a collection agent. It's a practical guide full of how to's, resources and advice — as well as insight into how she created a successful business that lets her balance family and work." –**Rebecca Joffrey, Co-editor of the book** *This Day: Diaries from American Women*

"I do enjoy your wisdom and approach to this industry, I try to steer more people to you who are getting into this industry." –**John Pratt, Portfolio Management LLC**

"Michelle Dunn is a tremendous resource, her books, web site, and forums continue to lead us through our new business in collections. We are very thankful for all her help." **Ken Keefe**

"Let me start by saying 'Thank you' for your book. It is yet another testament of the professional business woman you are. I believe in you and I will always contribute the success of my start-up to you. Thanks so much." – **Norma Burns, Burns & Carlisle**

"Thank you Michelle for your articles and representation of our industry! Your words are very eloquent and to the point. Keeping the business world aware of the value of third party collections is a constant in our business as often agencies receive bad press and we have to rebuild all over again. I enjoy your websites immensely!" –**Dan Jobrack, National Director, Fidelity National Credit Services Ltd.**

"I stumbled upon your site and LOVE IT! You write like a woman who has been in the industry the first site I have ever seen like that. I have found you to be an inspiration." – **Charlotte Kendrick Withrow**

"When I read your Second Edition of Starting a Collection Agency *I found it full of very good and lots of practical information, the writing is excellent."* – **David S. Osterman, General Counsel NeF Capital Group LLC**

"You out did yourself Michelle! Well worth the reading, effective and self comprehensive. Anyone can start their own collection business once they have sole possession of this book, which is packed with all the fixings, help-aids, resources, professional contacts, business set up information and best of all actual samples of proposals and more." – **Rollie McCarter, III, Rollie McCarter Investigative Services, Holyoke, MA**

DANIEL

Daniel didn't use *Starting a Collection Agency, how to make money collecting money* when he started thinking about opening his own debt collection agency. It took him over 3 years to open his doors with minimal clients and one employee.

ANITA

Anita did use *Starting a Collection Agency, how to make money collecting money,* and opened her agency in 6 months, with employees and a solid client base.

About the Author

Michelle Dunn has over 19 years experience in credit and debt collection. She is the founder and president of her Credit & Collections Association and Never Dunn Publishing, LLC, she is a writer, publisher, and entrepreneur. She was recently nominated as one of the Top 5 Women in Collections by Source Media out of NY and her Second Edition of Starting a Collection Agency won first place in the 2007 New York Book Festival Award in the "How to" category.

Michelle was named as one of Collection Advisor's Top 50 Most Influential Collection Professionals for 2007 as well as being nominated for a New Hampshire Business Review 2007 Business Excellence Award.

Michelle started M.A.D. Collection Agency in January 1998 and ran it successfully until she sold it in December 2004. She started, owns and runs Credit & Collections.com, a ten-year-old online association for credit and business professionals with thousands of members.

When you start your own company, you sacrifice your personal time, money, and effort in every way. Michelle has tried to sacrifice only her own time and not her children's time, by building and working at her business when they were in school, sleeping, or visiting their father. That way she could be there for them when they were home, or awake. Michelle has sold everything she owned to finance her business and the publishing of her books. She believes in herself and her success so she is not afraid to do this.

Michelle has had a great impact in her industry, showing women and men that they can start their own business, and helping them to do it. She created Credit & Collections.com, which has helped the industry to grow and learn. Her books, networking group, and website have helped her and others to be more successful. On a personal level this has been very satisfying for Michelle. She is happy to share her knowledge of what she has learned so others can be successful in this industry using the tools she can share. She had to research, create, and flounder through everything herself. Now she is able to provide that information to others so they can skip wheel reinvention and become successful quickly.

When she started her collection agency in 1998, debt collection was a field dominated by men. She joined the American Collectors Association when there were only 3 other women-owned agencies. Michelle joined and created networking groups for women in business, and served as the President of the Digital Women's New England Chapter for Women in Business. She could not find much information or help from others at that time so she created Credit & Collections (www.credit-and-collections.com), her own community for business people in the credit and debt collection industry. Dunn created a website to go along with it and an email discussion group. She still moderates this group and financially supported the website for over 10 years to network and help promote her members. She paid for everything and offered this as a free service to anyone. It is a highly regarded association, and she receives many thank you notes and emails from people who join, because it provides just what they are looking for. Debt collection is still dominated by men, but Michelle realizes that she has created many more agencies owned by women who have bought her books, joined her group and those she has personally mentored.

Michelle has tried to teach and help women, who have children and want to work but be there for their families, to realize that they can start a business from home. She tries to help them with marketing and promotion by including their information in her newsletters and on her websites for free, thus giving them advertising and exposure. She has sent free copies of her books to women who could not afford them. She will do anything to help a woman be successful and feel independent and proud. She thinks our children learn by our actions, so if they see their mother, creating and surviving by having her own business and working around her children, they see an empowered woman who puts her children first and foremost but can also be a success. Michelle is a member of "Women Inspiring Women" and donates her time, books and classes to this organization that brings business and professional women together to be successful.

Michelle has been repeatedly featured in The Wall Street Journal, Smart Money Magazine, Forbes.com, Ladies Home Journal, Home Business Magazine, Entrepreneur, Professional Collector, Credit & Collections Risk, the NH Business Review and in many business books. She has been a featured guest on (NPR) National Public Radio and has been in many newspapers and magazines nationwide as well as on the CBS Early Show, Process for Profit and The Book Authority. She has many published articles and 7 published books to add to her list of accomplishments. Michelle has written a book for Entrepreneur Press titled, *The Ultimate Credit & Collections Handbook, the check IS in the mail* as part of their Ultimate Series, which was released in October 2006.

Dunn was a member of the Plymouth Chamber of Commerce for 9 years and a member of The American Collectors Association for 9 years. She received a Certificate of Achievement from Credit Management Services for outstanding debt collections. She has a certificate of achievement from Dun & Bradstreet for Financial Analysis and Debt Collection. Dunn created and has been a member of Credit & Collections.com for 10 years. She has given speeches about debt collection and credit polices to business owners everywhere and she teaches non-credit courses on debt collection at Plymouth State University. She gives workshops sponsored by Micro-Credit of New Hampshire and is also a member of The New England Booksellers Association, SPAN, The Authors Coalition, New Hampshire Writers Project, the National Association of Women Writers and the International Women's Writing Guild.

She petitioned Governor Jean Shaheen for National Credit Week, and received a plaque and award from the governor's office. She has been named an Expert Author by Ezine Articles. She received a positive review from Writer's Digest and many other respected reviewers on her book ***Starting a Collection Agency,*** and has published a third edition. Starting a Collection Agency won first place in the how to category in the 2007 New York Book Festival.

Michelle Dunn is an outstanding representative of the business community in NH. Her entrepreneurial spirit, rugged individualism and resilience have made her a success in this community. She has managed to combine the roles of motherhood and business to an extraordinary level. Her drive and commitment separate her from any competition. She is a remarkable and unique woman who has found success through hard work and dedication.

Acknowledgments and Special Thanks

No book is ever written alone, and I want to thank everyone who has answered my questions, helped me with research, and supported my decision to educate people in this industry.

Thank you Nathan and Jonathan, Kevin Maass, Deb Berry, Cheryl Microutsicos, Britta Puffer, Betty Trought, Lourdes Lopez, David Ward, Robert Holt, Marcia Rosen, Cindy Dusseault, Carole Abel, Arlene Stoppe, everyone at the Plymouth Post Office, all of my friends and everyone in the credit and debt collection industry.

I want to sincerely thank all these people for being there.

Please note: Every effort has been made to assure this information is up to date and accurate as of publication date. It is not intended to be a full and exhaustive explanation of the law in any area. This information is not intended as legal or financial advice and may not be used as legal or financial advice. Please consult with your attorney, tax professional, and state and federal agencies to verify information for your individual situation.

TABLE OF CONTENTS

INTRODUCTION
WHY DID I WRITE THIS BOOK?

I published the first edition of *How to Make Money Collecting Money, Starting a Collection Agency* in 2002. I had started and been running my collection agency since 1998 and had gotten quite a bit of national press, with NPR and *Ladies Home Journal* and some other regional mentions. Once I was recognized nationally, I could not keep up with the emails, calls and postal mail from people who wanted to know how they could start their own agency and do what I was doing. I did some searching in bookstores and online and could not find any books on starting your own agency. I had looked for books on the subject in 1997 and 1998 to research for myself but didn't find any at that time either. Obviously there was a need for this type of book, and so I created one. That was my first book, and I have now had much more experience and can offer you even more help, suggestions and ideas on how you can successfully start your own collection agency, from an office or from a home office. Since I sold my agency, I now have time to also offer you consulting specialized to Starting a Collection Agency.

I can offer you experience and resources from having started my own home based business. I have over 20 years experience in business management and debt collection. I have been featured in *Ladies Home Journal, PC Magazine, Home Business Magazine, Home Business Journal*, on (NPR) National Public Radio and many other publications. I am a regular contributor to the *Wall Street Journal*, the *NH Business Review* and many other media publications. I have written and published 7 books on collecting money and starting your own collection agency and I have written *The Ultimate Book of Credit & Collections, the Check IS in the Mail*, which is being published by Entrepreneur Press as part of their Ultimate Series. It is available in bookstores nationwide, and online at Amazon.com.

When I started my business I did all my own research, read a lot of books, networked online and offline and took financial analysis and debt collection classes. I started my business with practically nothing and built it up to a successful home based business that I sold after eight profitable years. I have researched, done all the legwork and because of this experience, I know what mistakes you will make and can help you avoid them. I am confident I can help you start and run your own home based collection agency.

When you decide to use my consulting package, we will focus on the results that you are looking for. Once you tell me your needs, questions and concerns, we can come up with what results you want. We will then work together to achieve those results and I am confident they will be a reality.

The advantages of choosing me as your consultant are many. Something that would take you 20 hours to research, may take me 5 with resources I have readily available to me.

- You have support while you work.
- You will be inspired to do your best with my help.
- We can overcome challenges that might seem overwhelming to you alone.
- We can share ideas and make your dream a reality.

As your consultant I will help you determine what business you may want to start, what type of business might be reasonably feasible to you and your location. I will help you get information on any licenses or permits you may need, marketing, pricing, setting up your home office, dealing with interruptions, time and distractions, growing your business, increase sales, income and any questions you may have.

I will make recommendations to you on how you can save money while growing your business, inexpensive to free marketing ideas, and ways to promote yourself online and off.

Hiring a consultant to help you in the beginning stages of building your business will help you achieve success twice as quickly than if you tried to do it alone. If you do not wish to utilize my consulting, you can use this book as a guide and successfully start, run and grow your own debt collection business. I would highly recommend joining

Credit & Collections.com at www.credit-and-collections.com. I created the group because when I started my agency, I could not find any helpful networking groups in the credit field. There are now a few others and I have mentioned them in the Resources section of this book. If you ever come across any other resources that you love, please email them to me so I can include them in the next edition of this book and also so I can share them with the other members of Credit & Collections that are also trying to start or grow their agencies.

I am including an article I wrote titled "How a Woman became a successful Bill Collector in a "Man's Industry" and how you can too," because I think it will be helpful to you when you are making your decision to start your own agency. Anyone can start their own agency, man or woman, but being a woman, I wanted to share this with other women who may be thinking about starting their own agency.

"How a Woman became a successful Bill Collector in a "Man's Industry" and how you can too!"

I have worked in the credit industry for over 20 years now. When I first started out, I only knew a very few women in the industry. That number has grown over the years, but not by much. Being a bill collector has always been categorized as a "man's industry".

When I was a Credit Manager for other companies I worked for, I always did a great job, and collected more money than any other collector who held the job before me. I loved the job, I loved the challenge, and I loved that I could physically "see" my results by watching the bottom line of bad debt diminish. I once made a chart to bring to my performance review to show my boss how much more money they had and how much less bad debt and bad credit risks they had because of my efforts. I got to the point that I could not make any more money at these companies, as I was at the top of my pay for that position. I was also always bored. Once I had the credit situation under control, I wiped out my own job! So I started writing credit policies for the companies I worked for.

I started my own collection agency in 1998, without ever having worked at a collection agency. My experience was working in credit and being a bill collector for other companies. I did work with collection agencies, by placing accounts with them, and found a local agency that was very helpful and would network with me rather than see me as competition. I was very happy for that help and guidance, since most people did not think I would be successful. They obviously don't know me very well.

I did take courses through Dun & Bradstreet and also read every law book on credit and debt collection I could get my hands on. I joined the American Collectors Association and took advantage of everything they had to offer. I joined networking groups online and started my own networking group with a website www.credit-and-collections.com because I could not find a group or website in this field. Even though I have now sold M.A.D. Collection Agency, I maintain and moderate Credit & Collections and we have thousands of members as of the date of this writing.

I know that anyone can do anything they set their mind to. I did this because I wanted to be home for my children and have the flexibility to pick them up at school and go to school functions but still needed to support myself and my children. That will motivate you! If you have to keep working and get clients so you can buy groceries, you will.

No matter what you choose to do, if you are determined and keep learning, have drive and are motivated, as long as you are doing what you love and doing the best job you can do, you will be successful. For me it just happened to be collecting money.

Any one can do this job; you do need start up funds but not much. I started with a few thousand dollars and kept my day job until I had enough clients to quit. I then kept my day job as a client and did their collections as well. I started out doing everything manually, and then bought a computer; I still kept my files manually until I could purchase some low cost collection software. I did everything myself to save money, I learned marketing and sales and continued to educate myself on debt collection and new laws and changes in the industry every day. I know women who start this business at their dining room table. This is a hard job, and you have to be organized, have thick skin and be knowledgeable about collection laws and business in general. If you have kids at home you need to organize and make arrangements so you can make collection calls, be professional (without the dog barking in the background, or a child crying) and maintain your sanity when your kids are crying for your attention and the guy who just received your dunning notice calls you to explain to you that he wants to speak to the man in charge.

CHAPTER ONE
WHAT IS A COLLECTION AGENCY? AND CAN I MAKE MONEY DOING THIS?

What is the main difference between first-party and third-party debt collectors? Third-party collectors are directly regulated by the Fair Debt Collection Practices Act (FDCPA), which is enforced and administered by the Federal Trade Commission (FTC). The FDCPA sets forth guidelines to protect consumers from abusive, misleading and unfair debt collection practices. First-party collectors are the credit grantors or your clients, business owners who extend credit.

Third-party debt collectors work with First-party collectors or credit grantors to secure the payment of debts that have not been paid. As a professional debt collector you will locate consumers, determine why a bill or debt has not been paid and work with the debtor to get the payment. Unforeseen circumstances such as illness, death, job loss or divorce can sometimes cause an otherwise good credit risk customer to plunge into a situation where they cannot pay their bills.

A collection agency is a service business. Bill collectors act as agents for clients who could not get paid for products or services that they provided their customers. A business places past due accounts with an agency, and the agency tries to collect for them. Some agencies collect what is due on the bill and keeps a commission on what they collected, then sends the client the rest of the money. Some agencies charge a flat rate for collection efforts.

Agencies can collect for hospitals, physicians, lawyers, retailers, service providers and many other types of businesses. Any business that extends credit or accepts checks may have a need for a collection agency.

There are many laws an agency must follow when collecting debts. You should familiarize yourself with these laws and keep them for reference.

I include a listing of these laws later in this book, I also include a listing of what you can and cannot do when collecting money that is owed to your client.

Collection agencies have a terrible reputation caused by a few agencies that have created a bad name for the industry. This is why you should follow the FDCPA (Fair Debt Collection Practices Act) closely. Surprisingly, not all agencies follow the FDCPA.

Some collection agencies collect in different ways, some only collect by mail, some by mail and phone and some only institute legal action. You will need to decide which type of agency you want to start.

COLLECTION AGENCIES CAN COLLECT:

- Retail & Service debts
- Medical bills
- Bad checks, NSF, Account Closed
- Heating oil accounts
- Utilities
- Credit card debt
- Veterinary bills
- Loans

COLLECTION AGENCIES CAN PROVIDE:

- Asset searches
- Skip tracing
- Credit reporting
- Debt collection
- Demand letters
- Public record searches

COLLECTION AGENCIES SHOULD:

- Have experience in each of their specialized collection markets
- Be able to provide recovery percentages
- Be able to provide quality references
- Have a code of ethics that they follow

WHAT DO COLLECTION AGENCIES DO?

Collection agencies assist businesses and sometimes consumers in collecting money owed to them by their customers, tenants, or clients. All while encouraging a continuing relationship, though this does not happen often. This usually entails mail and telephone correspondence as the primary tools for reaching delinquent customers. Home based collection services have a distinct advantage in serving small businesses, particularly healthcare providers. Many large firms simply do not try to collect on smaller debts because it means less commission for the work and more time spent to make a small amount of money. However, home based collection agencies that specialize in small debts or do collections for small businesses are often successful.

HOW MUCH MONEY CAN I MAKE DOING THIS?

The majority of collection agencies do not get paid by the hour. Instead, they work on a commission basis, therefore if you do not collect, you do not get paid. Commissions range from 25 percent on young accounts to 50 percent on those that are older or a small amount. For instance, a collection service that gets the debtor to pay a $1,000 medical bill will earn $250 to $500 depending the age of the bill and the agreement with the business. Typical annual gross revenues range from $30,000 to $60,000, based on a 25 percent commission for collections of $10,000 to $20,000 per month (the average for a small collection service).

How do I know what to charge?

Setting your price is tough. You will want to research what other agencies in your area and nationwide are charging. Remember these tips:

Never set your price lower that what it costs to run your business.

If you have to increase your prices after starting your agency, offer another service or report that will make it worthwhile to the client.

Charge a lower price to start out with and raise prices later once you have happy clients and a reputation for quality work.

Remember when setting your price, ask yourself, what is my market going to pay and what are my costs? Remember to be competitive and not to charge to little. Charging to little could portray an image of less than quality work. Most clients will pay more for quality work.

NOTE–Child Support Collections: I have never done any child support collections but have had many people ask me about it, so I wanted to include this in here for you. I believe that collecting child support is a government enterprise, with its own DA office and deputies to serve warrants. I would contact your local District Attorney to see if this is a feasible option for you or your agency.

FYI: Studies show that smaller collection agencies have higher recovery rates. Studies done by *Credit Collection News* and *Credit Collections Directory* show that small collection agencies reported a 26% average annual recovery rate compared to the 17% rate reported by the largest collection agencies.

CHAPTER TWO
SHOULD I START MY OWN COLLECTION AGENCY?

SOME THINGS TO CONSIDER

There is nothing new about the fact that businesses often need help in collecting the money that is owed to them. One thing that seems common in the debt collection industry is that no one seems to leave. People seem to switch jobs but stay in the industry, myself included. There is a lot of money to be made in this industry if you are good at what you do and don't stop learning. Debt collection is a small community but one that is consistently growing and word will spread if you are good at what you do.

Something you want to remember when you think about starting your own debt collection agency is that there is a big difference between working for someone else and owning your own business, even if it is the same industry. When you own your own business you will work more hours and much harder then when you work for someone else. Some things to be aware of when you are considering starting your own agency are continuing education in the credit industry, making sure you have start up capital, learning and staying up to date on the federal and state laws in regards to debt collections.

Choosing to start a debt collection agency is an important decision and should be taken very seriously with much consideration.

You should have experience in the collection industry. I opened an agency when I had never worked at a collection agency. I had always been a Credit Manager, so I dealt with collection agencies. You must know what type of business the collection business is before you can understand what you are getting into. You need to know the day-to-day activities of collections.

You should also be ready to spend a lot of time getting people interested in your business. If you have worked in the industry for other people, new clients will know you have experience and be more comfortable placing accounts with you. You need to know the laws in the state you are in and the states you will be collecting in. You want to have experience dealing with people and good negotiation skills.

Write a business plan. If you are going to borrow money to start your agency you will need a business plan to show the bank. Usually a business plan is made up of:

- An Executive Summary
- A Business Description
- Marketing Strategies
- Competitive Analysis
- Operations and Management Plans
- Financial Statements

You should also include a cover or folder for your business plan. Include a title page and a table of contents. This will be very professional and impress any bank you may present it to.

You should love collection work. You either love it or hate it! If you love it, you will be passionate about making your business work.

Ask yourself, am I good at debt collecting? Am I good with people? You should have communication and investigative skills. Some other important skills of a bill collector are:

- Organization
- Empathy
- Negotiation
- Persistence
- Customer service skills

Be aware of what your potential clients will look for when choosing a collection agency to work with. If you can provide them with what they want and need, you have a better chance of becoming "their" agency.

Things to remember when starting up your agency

- Each collection market is handled differently. Be sure your agency has collections experience in credit union accounts, medical accounts or the specific interest of your potential client.
- Know your recovery percentages, not just the rate you will charge, to understand if your agency will deliver the best returns. For example if a client places $1000 for collection at 25% commission and you collect $300, they will receive $225. But if they place $1000 for collection at a 35% commission and then you collect $500, they will receive $325.
- Have a sheet of references, and if you can, post them on your website. Also, have a sheet or website page that shows any associations you belong to, let them know they can email or call those associations for a reference on your agency. Be clear on your collection methods and how you treat debtors. Some clients will place accounts with your agency that they wish to continue working with.

CHAPTER THREE

THINGS TO DO BEFORE YOU START YOUR AGENCY

When I started my collection agency my startup capital was $8000.00. Here is what I got for that money:

Computer
Printer
A new Desk, chair and chair mat
A used desk
Filing cabinets and supplies
Paper
Ink
Envelopes
Letterhead & business cards
Accounting software
Membership to my local chamber and ACA and Equifax
Paid for website hosting and a URL
Purchased folders and created my own promotional materials
Rented a postage meter
Telephone and phone services including voice mail
Business insurance
Fax machine and ink
Two phone lines
CD's and cases for backing up work
Copy machine and ink
Magazines and books about debt collection, starting a business and marketing
Office supplies
Paper shredder
Opened a PO Box

When I started out it was just me, no staff. I did not have staff for about 4 years and then it was part time help. I did not have debt collection software in the beginning, I used a tickler file and kept track of my accounts manually in a file cabinet. I learned all I could about marketing and site promotion since I could not afford to pay someone to do it for me. Joining associations helps get the word out about your agency, as does advertising. I advertised for the first 6 months and ran an ad in my local paper every other week to save money.

While you still have your "day job", there are some things you can do to prepare for when you run your agency full time. You should check out other collection agency websites and request their literature. Once you have gathered different packets of information from a few different agencies, lay it all out and look at what they provide to their potential customers. Then you can decide what you want to provide to your potential customers. You can get some great ideas here, if you don't see something you think is important, create it. If no one else is providing it, it will help you to stand out in the crowd.

With this information you can create your information packets that you will use to help sell your agency. I used red folders to hold my information, my company colors were red and white. So choose a color that compliments your business cards, websites or how you want to present your business. Here is an example of what I included in my information packets:

I used red folders from an office supply store that had a cut out for my business card; you can also paste your business card or a sticker on the front or inside.

On the left side I included	On the right side I included
Flyers on different services	Testimonials & references
(Skip tracing, letter service)	Collection Agreement
Skip tracing agreement	Rate sheet
Check collection flyer	Welcome letter
Brochure, postcard	When to Place accounts sheet

I have included examples of the above sheets and forms that you can use as a guide.

SKIP TRACING FLYER

Skip Tracing is the process of tracking someone who owes you money.

In order to successfully collect on a delinquent account, you have to locate the debtor. A debtor may relocate and/or have his telephone disconnected, believing they are leaving creditors with no immediate means of contact. However, skip tracing allows creditors to locate debtors through various outlets available to them.

A skip trace can be done for current address and phone, fictitious business names, social security death index, bankruptcies, judgments, liens, national property and deed transfers.

When should you skip trace?
◆ When mail is returned
◆ When the phone is disconnected
◆ When consumers stray and leave debts behind, follow in their tracks!

Some information needed for a professional Skip Trace

◆ Full name (first, middle, last)
◆ Social Security Number
◆ Date of Birth
◆ Former address
◆ Employment information
◆ Vehicle and drivers license information
◆ Spouse information
◆ All the information you have on file!

SKIP TRACING RATES
◆ FREE on accounts placed with us!
◆ Locate current address by Social Security number — Price: $25.00.
◆ Locate current address by telephone number — Price: $35.00
◆ Locate by name and state — Price: $40.00

RATE SCHEDULE FOR A/R OUTSOURCING

PROPOSED A/R RATES FOR:

Company Name

Based on the volume of an estimated 400 accounts per month, we can maintain these receivables for a flat monthly fee of $700.00. If the volume increases or you require additional work to be done, the fee will be adjusted.

The $700.00 monthly rate will include letters being sent and calls being made to resolve any disputes and obtain payment. This will be done on your letterhead and in your name and we will instruct all debtors/insurance companies to send payment directly to you.

We have a very high success rate with our Outsourcing program and are confident that you will see an increase in payments being sent to your office.

This agreement represents a legal binding contract between the Agency and Client. This contract remains valid unless terminated by either party with a ninety (90) day notice.

Please send boxes of letterhead and envelopes to:

My Collection Agency, PO Box 40, Plymouth NH 03222

Or send letterhead logos to my email

If you have return envelopes for the debtors to make payment in please send those as well. These help debtors to make more prompt payments and are even more effective if they are postage paid.

Agency:

My Collection Agency

Michelle Dunn/President _____ Date _____

Client:

Name of Company: _____

Type of business: _____

Signature _____ Date _____

Title _____ Email _____

SKIPTRACING AGREEMENT

This Collection Agreement, made this 6th day of January, 2006, by and between My Collection Agency, through the authorization of Michelle Dunn, President, hereinafter known as "Agency," and Babs Book Service, hereinafter known as "Client," sets forth the following terms and conditions:

The Agency agrees to:

Skip trace all accounts for a place of employment and for property.

The Client will only be charged a $10.00 fee on accounts that are a "hit".

If no homeowner confirmation or employment is found, The Client will not be charged.

The Client agrees to:

Send all accounts with a Social Security number via email in an Excel spreadsheet unless otherwise noted.

This Collection Agreement represents a legal binding contract between the Agency and Client, and all of its terms and conditions are enforceable by law. This contract remains valid unless terminated by either party with a thirty (30) day written notice.

Seen and agreed to as follows:

Agency:

My Collection Agency

Michelle Dunn/President _____ Date _____

Client:

Name of Company: _____

Type of business: _____

Signature _____ Date _____

Signature _____ Date _____

Title _____ Email _____

CHECK COLLECTION

What Can My Collection Agency Do for You? We accept every type of check for collections!

NSF

Account Closed

Refer to Maker

Stolen

Successfully collected checks pay you face value of the check

Customers are handled professionally

We work any age of check

Customers handled professionally

Prompt payment on collected checks

No cost to you

Note: Testimonials can be added after you have a few clients and you can ask them for a reference or if they are happy with your services, then create a sheet of the testimonials and include it in your packet. Also, post any testimonials on your website. An example would be:

"When I contracted your services, I had little hope of recovering the monies owed to me. It was extremely disheartening to have worked so hard, only for the client to ignore my requests for payment. As a last resort, I decided to place the account with your agency. I truly never expected to receive the payment.

Much to my surprise, not only did the company pay me after your contact with them, but they also placed other orders with me and agreed to pay up front until trust had again been established. More than that, I believe they have a respect for my business that they didn't have before. Your agency helped to instill a feeling of legitimacy, which as a home based business, is sometimes difficult to convey. "

COLLECTION AGREEMENT

This Collection Agreement, made this ____ day of _____, ____, by and between My Collection Agency, through the authorization of Michelle A. Dunn, President, hereinafter known as "Agency," and _____ hereinafter known as "Client," sets forth the following terms and conditions:

The Agency agrees to: Carry out all collection efforts in compliance with all applicable federal, state, and local laws.

Remit all monies collected to the Client along with their monthly statement.

Collection rate is 25% of what is collected. Accounts over one year old or under $75 are 50%. Second placements are 50%. Returned merchandise/ equipment as payment of claim: 50% of normal fee.

The Client agrees to: Report all payments, bankruptcy notices, and any communications from the debtor directly to the Agency upon the Client's receipt or knowledge of their existence.

Immediately stop all collection efforts by the Client, and to provide copies of any paperwork that will verify the debt, as requested by the debtor or Agency.

Pay any and all commission owed upon receipt of the Agency's monthly statement.

Pay any and all commissions owed to the Agency if:
- the Agency directly collects any monies due to the Client by the debtor on this account,
- the Agency finds that the account was previously paid by the debtor,
- the client withdraws the account after demand for payment has been made
- or The Client receives any monies directly from the debtor.

Payments made directly to you will be invoiced subject to the standard rates. My Collection Agency invoice payment terms are "Payable upon receipt"

This Collection Agreement represents a legal binding contract between the Agency and Client, and all of its terms and conditions are enforceable by law. This contract remains valid unless terminated by either party with a ninety- (90) day notice.
Seen and agreed to as follows:
Agency:
Title _____ Signature _____ Date _____
Client:
Name of Company_____
Title _____ Signature _____ Date _____

RATE SCHEDULE

Agency Name & Address

Phone & Fax

COLLECTION RATES

Collection rate is 25% of what is collected.

Accounts over one (1) year old or under $75.00 are 50%.

Second Placement accounts are 50%

Returned merchandise/equipment as payment of claim: 50% of normal fee

You will be charged if a debtor pays us or pays you directly. If the debtor pays *Agency*, we keep our commission and send you the balance. Payments are sent out monthly. If the debtor pays you, you must advise us IMMEDIATELY and we will invoice you for the commission. Reporting direct payments is required by law to avoid legal issues.

Payments made directly to you will be invoiced subject to the standard rates. *Agency* invoice payment terms are "Payable upon receipt"

SKIP TRACING RATES

FREE on accounts placed with us!

Locate current address by Social Security number — Price: $25

Locate current address by telephone number — Price: $35

Locate by name and state — Price: $40

To place an account for collection online or order a skip trace online go to www.myagency.com

Call for Pricing on our Letter Service and A/R Outsourcing Programs

January 1, 2006

Bobs Animal Hospital
P.O. Box 40
Plymouth, NH 03264

Dear Bob:
Thank you for choosing My Collection Agency for your collection needs!

By the time you receive this letter your debtor has already been contacted.

Enclosed is my card, please call or email me anytime you have any questions. I have also enclosed some other information on our services as well as a Collection Agreement.

Please fill out and sign the collection agreement and mail or fax it back to us.

Our fax number is (###).

Sincerely,
Agency

Signature/Title

January 1, 2006

Frank's Heating & Air Conditioning
123 Main Street
Chicago IL 60614

Dear Frank Brown:

Thank you for your interest in *Agency*!

When you place an account in our collection program we begin collection proceedings immediately. We charge a 25% commission on money that we collect, unless the debt is under $75 or over one year old then we charge a 50% commission on what we collect.

The enclosed "What to do when you receive a collection notice" pamphlet is sent to all customers with the initial collection letter.

We also handle collections on customers that are past due that you would continue to do business with, who need some basic collection action taken. This is done either as a collection account or in our A/R Outsourcing program.

To place an account with us, simply mail or fax the enclosed Collection Placement Form. You can also call in your information or e-mail it to michelle@myagency.com. To place accounts online go to www.myagency.com. You can also just fax or mail copies of bad checks, statements, invoices etc. The basic information that we need is name, address, phone and amount owed. We also offer credit reporting, skip tracing, A/R Outsourcing and a Letter Service for an additional fee.

At *Agency* we are certain we will more than meet your needs.

Sincerely,
Agency

Signature/Title

WHEN TO PLACE AN ACCOUNT WITH *AGENCY*
- The customer does not respond to the first invoice.
- Payment is not made within terms.
- The customer makes repetitious, unfounded complaints.
- The customer denies responsibility.
- The customer is a skip.
- The customer fails to keep in contact.

A COLLECTION AGENCY IS NEEDED IF A CUSTOMER IS:
- Habitually slow paying
- Skips, runs away from debt
- Tries to reduce debt through complaints
- Changes jobs frequently
- Does not return calls
- Rude and will not work with you
- Mail returned & phone disconnected

THE LONGER YOU KEEP AN ACCOUNT ON THE BOOKS, THE LESS CHANCE THERE IS OF COLLECTING IT. TO MAINTAIN CLOSE CONTROL OVER BAD DEBTS PLACE THEM WITH US ASAP!

Read all the books and magazines, e-zines and pamphlets you can about credit & collections. When you become a member of some trade organizations you receive collection magazines as part of your membership. Some other publications you may be interested in are:

Collector magazine. This magazine is a benefit of being a member of The American Collectors Association.

Creditworthy Company. Email Rich Hill at rich@creditworthy.com

Credit Risk Monitor. Visit www.creditriskmonitor.com for more information.

Kaulkin Media/Collection Industry.com. Visit www.collectionindustry.com for more information.

Collections & Credit Risk/Thomson Media. Visit www.thomsonmedia.com

Become the Squeaky Wheel, a Credit & Collections Guide for Everyone, by Michelle Dunn, available at www.michelledunn.com or amazon.com

Be sure to let any of these publications know that Michelle Dunn sent you!

You should also join online forums and subscribe to e-zines. I recommend my Credit and Collections Association. This association provides you with a free or paid membership depending on your needs and budget, and you can network with business people in the credit and collections industry. Credit and Collections has been around for more than 10 years and has thousands of members.

When you join my Credit and Collections Association, whether you decide on the free or paid Professional membership, you can share ideas, ask questions, gather information and network with other large and small business owners, entrepreneurs, and very knowledgeable people in the credit and collections industry. You will receive free information for your business, free promotion for your business and many free tools and forms for starting or running a debt collection agency. There are free e-books, and other books, e-courses and tools to help you educate yourself and your staff.

Other things you can do while you are setting up your agency, are to research and create a website. You might want to do it yourself to save money or hire someone to do it. Maybe you can barter with someone if you have no idea how to create a site. Check out other agencies websites and find out what they offer. Find out what clients look for in a website, one thing that is important to customers is immediate answers 24/7. If you have online payment options, online placement of accounts or email, those will keep people coming back to your site and make your job easier.

You can order or create your letterhead and business cards, research collection software, come up with your company name, and register it with your Secretary of State. Once you have registered your name, and receive the paperwork from the state with the gold seal you can open a bank account for your agency.

You will also want to apply for a Federal Employer Identification number using form S4; you can do that at www.irs.gov/pub/

If you are starting your own agency from scratch, and do not have any equipment, here are some things that you will need:

- a desk
- a comfortable chair, you will be spending a lot of time in it
- file cabinets
- a computer
- computer software
- answering machine or voice mail
- phone
- calculator
- miscellaneous paper supplies
- letterhead
- business cards and promotional materials
- CDs for backing up your work
- Internet connection
- Envelopes
- Brochures
- Printer

Some things you need, but don't have to purchase right away include a postage meter, copy machine, and fax machine. You can purchase stamps at the post office if you can't afford to rent a postage meter. Metered mail does, however, give a more professional appearance. You can also order pre-addressed, pre-stamped envelopes from the postal service. You can sometimes fax right from your computer, or fax from an office supply store for a fee. The same goes for making copies–you can pay a fee to have them made at an office supply store. If you are working in an office building with other businesses, sometimes you can share fax machines and/or copy machines for a fee. A good option is an all in one printer, fax, and copier.

When you first start your agency, you may keep track of your accounts manually or in your computer. At some point, as your business grows, you will want some type of collection software that can keep track of your accounts for you and has helpful features, such as a mail merge feature and a tickler system.

With all the desktop publishing options available, now you may be able to create and print your own business cards, brochures and fliers. This can save you a lot of money.

CHAPTER FOUR
SOFTWARE

COLLECTION SOFTWARE

Software spending for consumer collections will grow to $700 million by 2010 compared with $500 million in 2006 according to a report done by PayStream Advisors, a Charlotte, N.C., research and consulting firm. Many people are using software bought before the year 2000 and eventually will have to upgrade. If you have been researching debt collection software, you know that major software creators and vendors have been introducing products that can improve productivity, streamline actions and offering predictive tools. Some things to look for when researching software for your collection agency are:

Electronic placement of new accounts.
Acknowledgment of new accounts.
Reports updating clients on all accounts.
Electronic forwarding between agencies.
Skip tracing options
On-line capabilities for clients to view their accounts or run reports.

There are so many types of software you can purchase to keep track of your accounts. I used Abacus Totality when I first started out. This software is great for a small collection agency just starting out. It automatically calculates account balances, generates documents in Word or WordPerfect, has a full feature tickler system, has a variety of reports, is network ready, supports an unlimited amount of users, and my favorite, supports an unlimited number of debtor accounts. Contact Evan Zucker, ez@TotalitySoftware.com

I also used Collect! for Windows once my agency grew. I found this program to be very detailed and it certainly streamlines things for you. I never even used all the features before I sold my agency. Improve your cash flow with collection software that is easy to customize to suit your needs. Financial tracking and contact management are integrated into this flexible program. www.collect.org

CDS Collection Data Systems - Provides end-to-end hardware, software (finance, workflow, legal), RDBMS database and services interfaces (credit reporting, skip tracing, bankruptcy, ACH payment processing, dialer and voice recording, letters, accounting, email) in a package that reduces total cost of ownership by 50%. Contact John Piraino, johnp@cdstiger.com

CDS Inc.,
2225 First Street, Suite 102
Simi Valley, CA 93065-1983
phone: 805-527-9977

Columbia Ultimate - This software application specializes in debt recovery, collections and accounts receivable management. It automates all of your collection processes.

www.bluewaremedia.com - Judgment recovery software made in Access.

Remware Computer Systems, Inc. - Visit their website at www.remwarecs.com.

At Point, Inc. Debt Collection Software Solution http://www.atpoint.com/products.html Email George A. Gyure at george@atpoint.com and tell him Michelle Dunn sent you. At Point Inc. has used the following forms that Michelle Dunn specially provided for use in their product:
- Collection agreement
- Interest letter
- Proposal letter
- Request for payment
- Thank you letter

There are many collection software companies available. You can find most of them by doing a search on the internet for debt collection software or going to www.credit-and-collections.com.

*A note from Evan Zucker – Creator of Totality Software:

"When I started my solo collection practice in 1991 I was stymied by the lack of tools available to manage my cases and accounts. I represented a large San Diego collection agency, and I did all their legal collection work in the state of California.

At first I created an Excel spreadsheet to calculate interest and balances, but I quickly realized how impractical that was. Besides, it could not generate any reports, demand letters, or calendar reminders.

The only debt collection computer programs I could find were designed for large collection agencies and law firms with tens of thousands of accounts, and they cost thousands of dollars. As a solo practitioner, those programs didn't seem to make sense for me, but I realized I had no choice but to use some sort of software to automate my practice.

Eventually I bit the bullet and spent thousands of dollars on one of those programs. I quickly grew very frustrated because the program was so complicated that I couldn't figure out how to use it. The software publisher insisted that I needed to attend training sessions for a full week at its office on the other side of the country in order to learn how to use their program.

That wasn't very practical for a solo practitioner like me, and so I returned that program and bought another one. But the same thing happened – after spending thousands of dollars, I was stuck with another complicated and confusing program. I returned that program too and decided there had to be a better way.

I figured that if I was going to have to spend thousands of dollars for a collection program, I ought to get one that did what I wanted and was easy enough for me to use. So in 1995 I paid a local programmer to write a collection program just for my collection practice, and it worked great!

In fact, it was so great that I decided to see if other collection agencies and lawyers might be interested in an easy to use and affordable debt collection program. After all, I couldn't be the only collection professional who was fed up with the limited software choices. When I realized that there was a real demand for a program like mine, I decided to switch careers. I stopped practicing law, and I began selling the first version of Totality debt collection software in November 1995."

Collection programs such as Totality address the challenges faced by collection professionals, such as:

- Automate time-consuming tasks – prepare letters, documents and reports -
- Accurate financial calculations – interest, balances, contingency fees, pay-off amounts, amortization schedules, and principal/interest/cost splits
- Organize priorities and account details – client and creditor contact information, notes, and automatic reminders.

Today you're fortunate to have choices I didn't have when I started my collection practice. Here are some issues to keep in mind when you shop for collection software:

- Choose a program that allows you to start small and grows with your business.
- Select software that is easy to use and requires little or no training.
- Pick a software company that listens to its customers and enhances its product based on customer input.

While Totality is a good choice for people starting a new collection agency, there are many other collection software companies available.

ACCOUNTING SOFTWARE

I use Quicken for home and small business to keep track of my business account with my local bank, and for printing statements and invoices for clients. It also keeps track of who owes you money and their past due status. You can customize the invoices to include your logo. You can purchase Quicken at www.quicken.com or at a local office supply store.

With this software you can simplify your business taxes, keep track of accounts payable and receivable, create invoices and prepare reports. You can purchase checks to use with your Quicken software from Current or another check supplier. They are generally less expensive than purchasing them from your bank.

Other accounting software available is QuickBooks Pro 2000. You may want to check out different types to see what works best for you. Another one to try is www.peachtree.com

GENERAL BUSINESS SOFTWARE

You will want to have software that is compatible with your clients or potential clients. I have used Microsoft Office 2000 Small Business. This includes Microsoft Word, Excel, Outlook, Publisher, and many little extras. Many clients will want to send you documents in a Word format, or a listing of accounts to collect in an Excel format. You must be able to open them and be compatible. If not, the client may go elsewhere.

NETWORKING HARDWARE & SOFTWARE

If you have more than one workstation and need all of your computers to access your collection software or access the Internet with one Internet connection, you will need to network your computers.

Most business owners and homeowners now use wireless internet for all their needs. This is the easiest way to go and works great. You can get everything you need to create a wireless network for your home or office at your local computer or office supply store.

If you are going to accept files and emails from different people you will want some type of antivirus software. There are many types available, some of the more popular types are: Norton Anti-Virus, www.norton.com/ or McAfee www.mcafee.com/. You can download them from the websites and be notified when updates are available. You can also purchase them at an office supply store.

CHAPTER FIVE
THE BUSINESS PLAN

If you need financing for your agency, there are a few options. You can use a savings account, credit cards, investors, personal finances, IRA Accounts, family, or a bank loan. You can also check out www.sba.gov/financing/sbaloan/ for more options. If you will be applying for a bank loan, you will need a business plan. The plan needs to explain to the bank how the agency will generate income and how the loan be repaid.

ELEMENTS OF A BUSINESS PLAN FOR YOUR COLLECTION AGENCY

1. Cover sheet
2. Statement of purpose
3. Table of contents

    I. The Business
        A. Description of business and services
        B. Marketing
        C. Competition
        D. Operating procedures
        E. Personnel
        F. Business insurance
        G. Financial data
    II. Financial Data
        A. Loan applications
        B. Capital equipment and supply list
        C. Balance sheet
        D. Break-even analysis
        E. Pro forma income projections (profit & loss statements)
            Three year summary
            Detail by month, first year
            Detail by quarters, second and third years
            Assumptions upon which projections were based

F. Pro forma cash flow
    Follow guidelines for letter E

III. Supporting Documents
- A. Tax returns of principals for last three years
- B. Personal financial statement (all banks have these forms)
- C. In the case of a franchised business, a copy of franchise contract and all supporting documents provided by the franchiser
- D. Copy of proposed lease or purchase agreement for building space
- E. Copy of licenses and other legal documents such as
- F. Proof your agency is bonded.
- G. Copy of resumes of all principals
- H. Copies of letters of intent from suppliers, etc.

Some common errors made when writing a business plan follow. Try to avoid these problems:

- ◆ Important sections and/or subsections are missing.
- ◆ Page numbers do not match up correctly with the content of the plan.
- ◆ The table of contents is two pages in length when it could neatly fit onto one page.
- ◆ The table of contents provides too much detail and is cluttered.
- ◆ The text layout is not uniformly aligned and looks sloppy.
- ◆ It appears that little or no thought went into its design and creation.

THIS IS A SAMPLE COVER SHEET FOR A COLLECTION AGENCY

BUSINESS PLAN OF

Collection Agency

October 2000

This Business Plan contains confidential information and may not be copied or distributed without the written permission of

Collection Agency

Address/Phone

BUSINESS PLAN

STATEMENT OF PURPOSE:

M.A.D. Collection Agency's purpose is to provide collection services to other businesses. To help them collect on bad debts and avoid bad debts in the future.

BUSINESS DESCRIPTION:

M.A.D. Collection Agency was founded in January 1998 by Michelle A. Dunn to provide collection services and accounts receivable management tools to businesses. The Agency has many services to help clients collect money and avoid bad debt. The Agency offers collection help, accounts receivable outsourcing, skip tracing, credit reporting and a letter service.

MARKETING:

The Agency has hired a PR Agency to help in its marketing efforts.

M.A.D Collection Agency has also developed its own logo to achieve brand recognition for its service.

COMPETITION:

The Agency has sought out its competitors to work together in forwarding accounts or helping each other in business, so as to eliminate any sense of competition.

OPERATING PROCEDURES:

The Agency has a policy that all accounts placed are input and processed in the same day. Statements are sent to clients monthly along with all monies due.

You will want to write your business plan and approach your bank or investors about six months before the opening of your agency. Try to include enough money to "carry" your agency through at least two months of business. Some banks will want to see up to 6 months.

PERSONNEL

The agency screens all personnel before hiring and trains them in the aspects of collection laws, state laws and customer service through-out their employment with M.A.D. Collection Agency.

BUSINESS INSURANCE:

The Agency has business insurance, which was obtained through (Name your Insurance Company and include contact information).

FINANCIAL DATA:

M.A.D. Collection Agency maintains all accounts through a local bank and there are always sufficient funds to cover any monies collected for clients at any time.

LOAN APPLICATIONS:

If your bank gave you any loan applications, you would include them next in your business plan. Be sure to fill them out completely, accurately and neatly.

CAPITAL EQUIPMENT AND SUPPLY LIST:
- 4 Computers, stationary
- 4 printers/3 laser and 1 color desk jet, Envelopes
- 4 phones, Postage paid reply envelopes
- Fax machine, miscellaneous office supplies
- Letter folding machine, Brochures
- Postage meter and scale, Business cards
- Photo copy machine Promotional packets and materials
- Disks, CDs, backup materials
- Business checks
- Software

BALANCE SHEET:

You can print your balance sheet if you have it in your computer and add that here. If you have an accountant, they can provide you with your balance sheet. If you use a program like Quicken you can print these next few items out yourself.

BREAK-EVEN ANALYSIS:

This can also be obtained from your accountant or attorney or printed from your bookkeeping software.

PROFIT AND LOSS STATEMENTS:

Also obtain from your accountant or attorney or printed from your bookkeeping software.

THREE-YEAR SUMMARY:

Project how you think your business will do in the coming three years. Be very specific and give reasons why you feel it will do what it will do. This is where you write what your goals are and how you will obtain them.

Break it down by month for the first year; for example:

In January of 2001 we will do a direct mailing of 40,000 pieces to hospitals and medical offices in effort to obtain 1,000 new medical collection clients. In February 2001 we will offer a free letter service to 20,000 retail businesses in effort to gain 2,000 new retail clients.

For your second and third year, give details by quarter. Also, be sure to explain why you think these projections will work. Be very specific.

CASH FLOW:

Project what you think your business will have for cash flow. Use the guidelines from your three-year summary. Be sure to explain why and how you think you will meet certain cash flow amounts. If you have a credit policy plan (See *Become the Squeaky Wheel, a Credit & Collections Guide for Everyone*, by Michelle Dunn) you would add that information here.

SUPPORTING DOCUMENTS:

◆ Include copies of the following:
◆ Tax returns for the principals of the business for the last three years
◆ Personal financial statement (you can get a form from your bank to fill out for this)

- If you are a franchise, include a copy of your franchise contract
- Copy of your lease for where your office location is or will be
- Copies of your collection license, proof of insurance and proof that you are bonded
- Copies of resumes for all principals of the agency
- Copies of letters of intent from all suppliers, such as the printer producing your letterhead, business cards, brochures, your computer support company, the company from whom you rent your postage meter

Shop around for the best interest rate and terms

Get your financing before you open your agency or sign a lease

Get everything in writing

Hire an accountant or attorney to review any agreements before signing

Check for a prepayment penalty

CHAPTER SIX

LEGAL REQUIREMENTS

FORM OF BUSINESS

You will probably be opening the agency with just yourself at first, so it could be a Sole Proprietorship. You can also operate as a partnership, limited partnership, corporation or limited liability company.

Sole proprietorship is usually the easiest and most common when opening a business. You will need a business license and maybe a fictitious name filing with the county clerk. Call your local county clerks office to find out.

There is a disadvantage to being a sole proprietor. Creditors can attach your personal property, or any other assets you have and possibly ruin your personal credit if you become past due on any business related bills or if you close the business.

Once you create this entity, you attract the attention of the government. If your business makes a profit, the various tax agencies want tax filings and payments. The taxes a sole proprietor will pay and the forms needed are:

- Income tax Form 1040 & Schedule C or C-EZ
- Self-employment tax 1040 & Schedule SE
- Estimated tax 1040-ES

If you have a partnership, both partners are liable for the others' actions. If there is ever any legal action, both partners will be sued personally. If one partner bows out, the other partner is left having to deal with the business left behind. You should consult an attorney when forming a partnership to draw up a partnership contract. The taxes a partnership will have to pay and the forms they will need are:

- Annual return of income Form 1065
- Employment Taxes 1040 & Schedule SE

- A partner in a partnership (individual) will need to file Income Tax Form 1040 & Schedule E
- Self-employment tax Form 1040 & Schedule SE
- Estimated tax Form 1040-ES

You can also set up a corporation. A corporation is totally separate from any of your personal assets. It is legally responsible for all debts and actions and you are considered an employee of the corporation. You will want to consult an attorney to have them help you file corporate papers. If you form a corporation two entities will be taxed, yourself and your business. A corporation is an independent taxable entity. When your corporation has an income, it owes a corporate tax. If you form a corporation you will also need a federal tax ID number.

A corporation will have to pay the following taxes and need the following forms: Income tax Form 1120 or 1120-A (corporation) Form 1120S, for an S Corporation Estimated tax Form 1120-W (corporation only and Form 8109 Employment taxes Form 941 and 940)

If you decide to form a limited liability company you will not personally be responsible for the businesses debts. Not all states have passed LLC legislation.

The 18 states that offer this are Arizona, Colorado, Delaware, Florida, Iowa, Kansas, Louisiana, Maryland, Minnesota, Nevada, New Hampshire, Oklahoma, Rhode Island, Texas, Utah, Virginia, West Virginia, and Wyoming. Several other states are considering LLC legislation.

If you decide to form an LLC you must file certain papers with an official in your state, and you will also need a federal tax ID number. The LLC works like a partnership with the liability protection of a corporation. You may also set up an S Corporation. If you have a family business or a business that does not require a great deal of equity from investors this might be for you. There are limits to the number and type of share-holders in an S Corp. Each shareholder must be a U.S. Citizen or resident alien and must be a natural person. An S Corp. cannot own more than 80% of another corporation. There are also different types of businesses, such as insurance and financial companies, that cannot qualify for S Corp. status.

If you do qualify as an S Corp. it is not the tax equivalent of a partnership. The tax implications are generally the same as for a limited liability company (LLC). One of the disadvantages of forming an S Corp. is that if your S Corp. has passive income (rent, royalties, etc.) that exceed 25% of gross receipts, you may be hit with the so-called "sting tax." Seek out good tax advice when forming your company.

◆ The taxes you will need to file and forms needed are:
◆ Income tax Form 1040 & Schedule E
◆ Estimated tax Form 1040-ES

Some websites that can help you with your small business tax questions:

◆ State Tax forms: www.1040.com/state.htm
◆ IRS Online: www.irs.ustreas.gov
◆ Intuit: www.qfn.com

To obtain the forms for a Sole Proprietorship, LLC, Partnership or Limited partnership, contact your State offices or visit their websites. You can now download all the forms you need and mail them in with a check.

CHAPTER SEVEN
LICENSES AND REGULATIONS

LICENSES, BONDING, AND ZONING

In many states there are required bonds, insurance or licensing. The amount or need for each is regulated by your states statute. The bond requirement is kept on file with your state and used if funds are not paid to your client. A bond is different from your insurance in that the owner of the agency agree to pay back any losses that arise from any claims against the bond.

Most agencies carry Error and Omission Liability insurance, or general liability, workers compensation and sometimes commercial crime insurance. Talk to your peers, ask industry professionals and find out what is best for your situation.

Avoid getting into trouble by researching and learning all you can about your states requirements including any special text requirements for collection letters, statutes of limitations, responsibilities of husbands and wives in regards to each others debts, the responsibilities of minors for their own debts, your rights and your clients rights under bankruptcy proceedings and judgments in your state.

Some states require a collection agency to have a state license and/or to be bonded. Some states do not require any license or bonding. Be sure to check what is required in your state before you start your agency. You may also need a business license in your city. Check with your planning or zoning department to make sure the zone covering your property is allowed and meets all codes.

If you want to run your agency from your home, you will have to find out the zoning ordinance for your area. Contact your town clerk and ask for a copy of any ordinances concerning home based businesses.

CODES & ACTS

You will also want to be familiar with certain codes and acts that help you follow the laws on collections.

The Robinson Patman Act (1936) This act makes it illegal to discriminate among customers on the basis of price if it would injure competition among sellers. This means the cash discounts for customers who pay promptly are legal. Discounts for customers who buy from another company are illegal.

The Assignment of Claims Act (1940) This act permits the assignment of proceeds from contracts to institutions solely involved in banking or financial activity. In effect, this allows businesses to replenish their supply of operating capital immediately on shipment of a product and opens the door to receivables financing.

Uniform Commercial Code (1972) This provides the basis for all commercial transactions. Of particular interest to you as an entrepreneur are Articles 4 (bank deposits and collections) and 9 (secured transactions, sales of accounts, and chattel paper).

The Fair Credit Reporting Act (1970) This regulated consumer credit information in regard to the confidentially, accuracy, relevancy, and proper utilization of customers' credit histories.

The Equal Credit Opportunity Act (1977) Prohibits discrimination on the basis of sex or marital status in granting credit.

The Fair Debt Collection Practices Act (1977) This eliminates abusive collection practices by debt collectors. The Federal Trade Commission governs this law.

Postal Regulations; This legislation required that no words, illustrations or codes identifying an addressee as delinquent in payment of a debt may appear on the outside of an envelope or postcard where they might be seen by a third party.

Internal Revenue Service; The IRS governs writing off bad debts.

State regulations; Each state has its own laws regarding collection processes.

Check with your towns zoning commission for restrictions that will limit your collection operations. Ask if there will be any known changes that will affect your business.

CHAPTER EIGHT
WHERE TO FIND CLIENTS

One of the first things you will want to do even before you open your agency is to obtain new clients to place accounts with you. The first step to doing this is to get your name out there. Use all your personal contacts and networking opportunities to do this. Join and participate with local and national groups and associations, volunteer at community events, have a marketing plan and stick to it, use direct mail, list your business in the yellow pages.

When networking be sure to be specific when describing your services, be friendly and positive and follow up with potential prospects.

Now your agency is all set up. You have a computer, letterhead, business cards and a phone. How do you find clients to place accounts with you?

NEWSPAPERS

One of the most successful ways I found potential clients was looking through the want ads in the newspapers. I looked for any business that needed help in accounts receivable or needed a credit manager or bookkeeper. The ad usually had an address, phone number, and sometimes a fax number. I created a flyer with my information and sent it to them with my business card. Then I called them a few days later, to see if they received my flyer and if they needed my services.

I made a list of all these companies each week and created a mailing list for direct mail. Keep in mind the average person has to see something approximately six times before they may act upon it. So don't get discouraged if your phone doesn't start ringing off the hook right away.

You also want to make your flyer stand out so that it gets noticed. You can do this by using colored paper, a catchy headline, a colored envelope or different size envelope, or by enclosing something unusual in the envelope.

CREATIVE FLYERS

I once made up a flyer on colored paper and enclosed children's play money inside. I had a lot of response from that. I even had people call to tell me they didn't need an agency but wanted to tell me how everyone in their office got a big kick out of the flyer with the play money. Agency owners who have used this book to start an agency have told me that this also has worked extremely well for them. If you are a member of your chamber of commerce, ask about inserting your flyer in their newsletter. Most will do this for a small fee. Also hang flyers up on public bulletin boards in your town and in shop windows.

DOOR TO DOOR

You can also just go door-to-door to local businesses. Make a list of businesses that you think may need your service. Get dressed up, put together your promotional packets and extra business cards, and visit them. You can leave your materials and sometimes get a name of someone who is in charge of the receivables. Then go back another time, perhaps bringing donuts or pens or some little promotional item. I have had great luck with this also. Remember: People like to do business with people they know and like.

BUSINESS ORGANIZATIONS

Join your local Chamber of Commerce, the Rotary Club, or any area networking groups. You can also join online communities for networking opportunities. Some are targeted just for the credit and collections professionals. One site I created is credit-and-collections.com and there is also www.creditworthy.com. There are also organizations for women business owners, such as NAFE www.nafe.com, Digital Women www.digital-women.com, and Women Inspiring Women www.wiwnh.com.

These organizations have resources for starting your business, marketing, getting customers and many other things you will need to get your agency off the ground.

REFERRALS

Once you get a few customers, ask them for referrals. If they are happy with your service, this will be the next best way you get business. Happy clients will tell other business owners about you, especially if you are sending them money!

If you collect on returned checks you can also target retail stores or anyone who accepts checks as a form of payment.

TIP: Understand your business and your customers needs, know who your potential customers are.

CHAPTER NINE

PROPOSALS

CREATING A PROPOSAL

If you have a potential client to whom you want to send a proposal, this will help you to get one together. I always typed my proposals on bright white paper and bound them in thin binders with clear covers or report covers.

You want to include information such as:
- An introduction letter
- Collection Agreement
- General Information
- Services
- Internet Capabilities
- Payment Options
- Skip Tracing Capabilities
- Forwarding Information
- Direct Mail & Telephone calls
- NSF Check Collection
- Legal Action
- Qualifications
- Costs

Also include information on any other services you may be providing them, such as:
- Credit reporting
- Letter services
- Accounts receivable outsourcing

SAMPLE PROPOSAL LETTER

October 12, 2006

Client's name Address

Dear:

It is my pleasure to submit this proposal to (company name) for your consideration. I am confident you will find our qualifications and our delinquent account recovery strategically mapped out. I believe this is a plan that will greatly reduce your overdue accounts, while maintaining a respectful relationship with your clients.

We have a reputation for having a fair and effective approach to handling delinquent debtors while maintaining their dignity and respect. This, above all, makes us the best choice in account recovery.

Feel free to ask any questions or to inquire about details of any of the information herein. I look forward to hearing from you soon, and starting the process to minimize your past due balances.

Sincerely,

My Collection Agency

The Best Ways to Get Business

◆ Directly solicit potential clients by phone and in person.

◆ Networking

◆ Speaking and attending seminars

◆ Send out press releases

◆ Be available for the press

◆ Write articles

◆ Have a website and promote it online and offline

SAMPLE PROPOSAL INFORMATION

GENERAL INFORMATION

(Agency) confirms that all costs quoted inside this document for services are not in excess of those which would be charged to any other individual or entity for the same services, performed by this agency.

(Agency) operates under and adheres to all Equal Opportunity laws and regulations set forth by federal and state statutes.

(Agency) is a professional, full-service agency, ensuring quality results for our clients while maintaining the dignity and respect of the debtors. The excellent performance and reputation of (Agency) are the major reasons why we are the absolute best choice in account recovery.

SERVICES

- Collections
- Direct Mail & Telephone Calls
- Non-Sufficient Funds (NSF) Check Collection
- Legal Action
- Skip Tracing
- Letter Service
- Accounts Receivable Outsourcing
- Credit Reporting

INTERNET CAPABILITIES

(Agency) is online and at your service. With our Internet capabilities, (Client) can utilize a popular and growing form of communications. (If you offer any other online services, list them here, also list your email address.)

PAYMENT OPTIONS

Payments can be received in various ways including, but not limited to, checks or money orders received by mail, checks by phone, checks or cash picked up at the debtor's residence or place of business, or credit cards.

SKIP TRACING

Accounts needing skip tracing will be subject to, but not limited to, city and rural directories, credit bureau inquires, nationwide electronic directories as well as data base searches of address, phone, social security numbers, driver's license number, similar names and places of employment.

FORWARDING

Accounts will only be forwarded if the debtor has moved out of state and it has been determined that the chances of collection will increase by doing so.

DIRECT MAIL & TELEPHONE CALLS

A letter will be sent out to the debtor immediately after the account is assigned to (Agency) describing the account balance and what the debt is for. A phone call will be made once the debtor receives the initial letter. Additional letters and phone calls will be made as required. (You can specialize this to be very specific to your agency.)

NSF CHECK COLLECTION

(Agency) will send a "demand for payment notice" on all insufficient funds or account closed checks written and received by either (Agency) or (Client) requiring the face amount of the check and a reasonable handling fee to be paid. Checks returned to (Client) for any other reason (i.e. lost or stolen, stopped payment or refer to maker) will be entered into the system and a letter sent. (Agency) will then verify the reason for non-payment and pursue with collection efforts.

LEGAL ACTION

When necessary legal action may be needed to collect an account. After meeting a strict pre-legal action criteria, a request for authorization to take legal action will be made to (Client) on those accounts. The request will be made in letter format to (Client) for authorization.

QUALIFICATION

List any associations your agency belongs to here.

List any awards or specialized collections you do.

(Agency) will exercise its best, prudent, and lawful efforts to secure collection of all accounts, including any NSF checks presented, regardless of amount, referred by (Client). Collection activities would include letters, phone calls, skip tracing, credit reporting, legal action and any other collection activity necessary to collect accounts. All collection and reporting activities will be in strict compliance with all applicable federal, state and local laws. Should there be any changes in the law (Agency) will modify its methods accordingly. (Agency) will be solely responsible for complying with all the aforementioned laws and regulating collection enforcement methods.

COSTS

List all of your fees here for all the services that you provide, be very specific.

CHAPTER TEN

GENERAL MARKETING INFORMATION

WHO ARE YOUR POTENTIAL CLIENTS?

You will need to market your agency to get clients. You first need to know who your potential clients are. Who do you want as a customer?

You can look in your yellow pages. Any business that extends credit may need your service, including banks, oil companies, contractors, florists, printing companies, doctors offices, dental offices and more.

WHAT METHODS SHOULD YOU USE TO MARKET YOUR BUSINESS?

You then need to decide what methods you want to use to market your business. Do you want to do direct mailings, put an ad in a local paper, put ads in magazines? What is your budget? How much can you spend on your marketing campaign?

What message do you want to come across in your marketing materials? You want these businesses to use YOU to collect their money! You want to let them know what services you are offering, the quality of your service, and how you compare with the competition. You also want to advertise or be seen regularly and continuously.

Two of the most important things in marketing your agency are patience and follow-up.

RESEARCH YOUR POTENTIAL CLIENTS

Research who you want as a client. They are probably already using an agency, so try to find out more about the agency they are using and what the client's needs are. Then follow-up and tell them what you can offer, offer them something that you know they are not getting now. Also, ask them what would they like to know about your agency or about you, and what would make them try out your agency.

If you don't follow up the client may think you are not really interested, or that if you aren't persistent with them, you may not be with debtors.

MARKETING TIPS

Marketing is one of the most important things you do for your business. A common mistake new entrepreneurs make is thinking that they only have to market their business in the beginning to obtain new customers and get their business off the ground. You have to market your business every day–forever. Here are some things you can do to help you in your marketing endeavor:

- Networking - join a chamber of commerce or rotary club
- Give speeches or seminars
- Volunteer at local events
- Create a gift certificate or coupon
- Make yourself newsworthy by holding a contest or sponsoring an award
- Ask existing customers for referrals
- Advertise in a local paper and online
- Write articles and columns and post them on your website
- Send out direct mail in an unusual or lumpy package, include a sample
- Write press releases and submit online and to your local media
- Write articles and submit to online sites

The Federal Trade Commission has strict rules on when a business can use the telephone for soliciting customers. Violation of these rules can result in a fine. The rules are:

- Call only between 8 a.m. and 9 p.m.
- Inform the customer that it's a sales call
- Describe the goods or services you're selling
- If there is a prize involved, explain the odds of winning and that no purchase if required to win

Marketing can be a fun part of your business day. Make sure to do at least one thing to market your business every day. Don't get discouraged! It can take months, or even years, to see results from your marketing efforts. I once obtained a new customer, which was the result of my visiting their office over a year before and leaving a folder of my information!

Other ways to market your agency include:

◆ Introducing new products or services (Remember to send out a press release!)

◆ Add a new state or specialized type of collection to your agency (obtain a license in another state or add credit card debt to your collections)

◆ Bundle collection products or services at a special price (maybe a letter service?)

◆ Refine or update a service you currently offer (more frequent updates or reports)

Tips for obtaining new clients:

Know your business and your potential customers needs

Know who your potential customers are and where they are

Implement a marketing plan

If you need to research demographics, visit these sites:

www.census.gov/ US Census Bureau

www.fedstats.gov/ FedStats

www.bls.gov/ United States Bureau of Labor Statistics

www.demographicsnow.com Demographics Now

MARKETING PLAN OUTLINE

◆ Analyze the total market for your service. Figure out which aspects of your service will appeal to different market segments.

◆ Define your services and list the features and benefits in detail. Also explain how it is different from the competition. You must be able to explain your product, and your competitor's product, then explain why yours is better.

◆ Form a marketing message and "tag line." For example, M.A.D.

Collection Agency's tag line was "We Turn Bad Debt Into Profit!" Describe how your service will benefit your clients.

- Create a pricing schedule or rate sheet. Do you offer discounts and if so, to whom do you offer them?
- What media will you use for marketing?
- Make sure your marketing materials mention any added services that they might not know you offer.

Description of the target market
- How long in business
- Type of business
- Income level
- Number of employees

Description of competitors
- Market research data
- Demand for product or service
- Nearest direct and indirect competitors
- Strengths and weaknesses of competitors
- Assessment of how competitor's businesses are doing
- Description of the unique features of your service
- Similarities and dissimilarities between your
- service and competitors

Description of service
- Describe your services
- Emphasize special features, i.e., the selling points

Marketing budget
- Advertising and promotional plan
- Costs allocated for advertising and promotions
- Advertising and promotional materials
- List of advertising media to be used and an estimate of cost for each medium

Description of location
- Description of the location
- Advantages and disadvantages of location

Pricing Strategy

- Pricing techniques and brief description of these techniques
- Competitive position
- Pricing below competition
- Pricing above the competition
- Multiple pricing
- Service components
- Material costs
- Labor costs
- Overhead costs

CHAPTER ELEVEN
THE MARKETING PLAN

MARKETING PLAN EXAMPLE #1

This is the marketing plan of:

Collection Agency

Address/Contact

I. MARKET ANALYSIS
   A. Target Market - Who are the customers?
      1. We will be selling primarily to:
         Total Percent of Business
         a. Private sector   10%
         b. Wholesalers   10%
         c. Retailers   10%
         d. Government   0%
         e. Medical   30%
         f. Service business   40%
      2. We will be targeting customers by:
         a. Product line Services
      3. We will target specific lines of Bad debt collection
         b. Geographic area? Which areas? New Hampshire
         c. Sales? We will target sales of our collection services
         d. Industry? Our target industry is service businesses
         e. Other? _____
      4. How much will our selected market spend on our type of product or service this coming year?
         $45,000
   B. Competition
      1. Who are our competitors?
         NAME Guetto's Bad Collections
         ADDRESS 1 Pain Place, New York, NY 10000
         Years in business: 15
         Market share: 10%
         Price/Strategy: 75%

Product/Service Features: Uses baseball bats
2. How competitive is the market?
High _____
Medium __X__
Low _____
3. List below your strengths and weaknesses compared to your competition (consider such areas as location, size of resources, reputation, services, personnel, etc.):
Strengths/Weaknesses
Follow the FDCPA/New to the industry
Member of American Collectors Association
Name not well known
Follow all state laws /No clients as of yet
Not discouraged easily/No name recognition

C.   Environment

1. The following are some important economic factors that will affect our service (such as country growth, industry health, economic trends, taxes, rising energy prices, etc.):

Being in a rural area, we must expand our marketing through out the state and surrounding areas. With new business growing in the rural area, there is potential to pick those new businesses up as clients.

2. The following are some important legal factors that will affect our market:

New bankruptcy laws and collection laws. We keep up to date on these laws by being a member of The American Collectors Association.

3. The following are some important government factors:

4. The following are other environmental factors that will affect our market, but over which we have no control:

Recessions or loss of jobs or factories that supply many jobs to folks in this rural area.

II. Product or service analysis

A.   Description

1. Describe here what your service is and what it does:

We offer debt collection services for businesses, skip tracing services to locate debtors, and credit reporting services. Our service helps businesses recover money they may have otherwise have had to write off to bad debt.

B. Comparison

1. What advantages does our product/service have over those of the competition (consider such things as unique features, patents, expertise, special training, etc.)?

Since we are a local agency we can make personal visits to debtors which an out of state agency cannot do. No other agency in the general vicinity offers this.

2. What disadvantages does it have? It take us out of the office when we could be making more collection calls or sending more collection letters.

C. Some Considerations

1. Where will you get your materials and supplies?
Babs Printing Palace
Staples
Office Depot

III. Marketing strategies/market mix

A. Image

1. First, what kind of image do we want to have (such as cheap but good, or exclusiveness, or customer oriented, or highest quality, or convenience, or speed, or ...)? High quality, convenient and fast.

B. Features

1. List the features we will emphasize:

a. Fast service

b. Determination

c. High quality (following FDCPA)

C. Pricing

1. We will be using the following pricing strategy:

a. Competitive __X__

b. Below competition ____

c. Premium price _____

d. Other _____

    2. Are our prices in line with our image?

       YES __X__ NO _____

3.   Do our prices cover costs and leave a margin of profit?

       YES __X__ NO_____

D.   Customer Services

    1. List the customer services we provide:

       a. Fast turn around on placement of accounts

       b. Monthly updates

       c. Monthly remittance of monies collected

    2. The competition offers the following services:

       a. Free letter service

       b. Lower rate on older accounts

E.   Advertising/Promotion

    1. These are the things we wish to say about the business:

       We turn your bad debt into profit, Place accounts for Fast turnaround, Convenient placement of accounts

    2. We will use the following advertising/promotion sources:

       a. Television _____

       b. Radio _____

       c. Direct mail ___X____

       d. Personal contacts ___X____

       e. Trade associations ___X____

       f. Newspaper ___X____

       g. Magazines __X_____

       h. Yellow Pages ___X____

       i. Billboard _____

       j. Other_____

    3. The following are the reasons why we consider the media we have chosen to be the most effective:

For local customers, the newspaper and yellow pages are things they may turn to when they need an agency. Trade associations add credibility to the agency, especially when it is a new business. Personal contacts put a name to the ad in the newspaper or magazine and help develop the customer/client relationship.

MARKETING PLAN EXAMPLE #2

1. Collect names and location information for businesses you want as clients.
    a. Use office directories for buildings in close proximity to your office
        i. Verify information, names, titles etc.
        ii. Phone the office and get the name of the billing or A/R supervisor
2. Send an introductory letter to that contact which introduces your company and ask for a meeting.
3. If you do not get a response to your request for a meeting, drop by.
    a. Drop by with a promotional item, business card and packet of information about your services and fees.
    b. Follow up.
4. Repeat as necessary.

CHAPTER TWELVE
FAIR DEBT COLLECTION PRACTICES ACT

For more information on the FDCPA you can find it online and also in my book, *Become the Squeaky Wheel, a Credit & Collections Guide for Everyone*, ISBN# 0970664516 $29.99 available at www.michelledunn.com or www.amazon.com. *Become the Squeaky Wheel, a Credit & Collections Guide for Everyone* also includes the FCRA if you will be doing any credit reporting.

The Three major Credit Bureau's are Equifax, Experian and TransUnion. You can sign up with all or one of them to do credit reporting. Of the three, TransUnion has the lowest minimum requirements at 100 accounts a month. The others have a minimum of 500 a month. You can submit accounts online through their websites or through Electronic Data Transmission over the internet.

FAIR DEBT COLLECTION PRACTICES ACT INFORMATION

In 1976 the Federal government passed a law to protect consumers from unfair debt collection practices. This law does not apply to businesses, but rather to collection agencies, and sometimes attorneys.

- You cannot call the debtor during unusual hours, such as Between 9 p.m. and 8 a.m. You can call during this time if you have the debtor's permission or if you know they will only be home during these times because of a work schedule.
- If the debtor has retained an attorney, you must speak only to the attorney.
- You cannot call the debtor at work if they ask you not to, or if the employer tells you not to.
- You cannot call the debtor's friends, neighbors, and relatives to collect the money. You can call them once to verify a debtor's location.
- You cannot use postcards to collect a debt. They reveal any message that would let others know you are trying to collect a debt.

- Your return address on the envelope of any correspondence to the debtor cannot indicate that you are a debt collector.
- You cannot use violence or the threat of violence.
- You cannot use obscene or profane language.
- You cannot distribute lists of debtors.
- You cannot advertise the debts.
- You must identify yourself at the beginning of the collection call, name and company.
- You cannot call the debtor with the intent to harass. Such as calling back after the debtor has hung up on you and causing the phone to ring endlessly.
- You cannot use a false name.
- You cannot report false information to the credit bureau. If the debt is disputed it must be reported as such.
- You cannot lead the debtor to believe you are an attorney or in any way related to the government.
- You cannot send letters that look like court documents or legal documents.
- You cannot lead the debtor to believe he has committed a crime in not paying a bill.
- You cannot misrepresent the debt, or lie about the debt.
- You cannot threaten any action you don't intend to take, such as court action.
- You cannot call a debtor collect.

SOME THINGS TO REMEMBER

A debt collector can mention "legal action" to a debtor or consumer when attempting to collect a debt if the debt collector intends to take that action. You can only state you will take legal action if you have the authority to take that action. This is also sometimes referred to as "further action".

If you report debts to the credit bureaus you can notify the debtor or consumer that a non-payment will affect their credit record. If you do not report to the credit bureaus, you cannot state this.

What does the FDCPA consider "unfair?"

- Collecting any amount of money that is not authorized by the agreement or contract that created the debt, or that is permitted by law.
- Accepting a check or other type of payment that is postdated more than 5 days unless you notify the debtor or consumer in writing of your intent to deposit said payment.
- Soliciting or asking for a post dated payment with the intent to deposit and then threaten prosecution for a "bad check".
- Collect telephone calls to the debtor or consumer.
- Collect telegrams to the debtor or consumer.
- Threatening repossession if there is not an option or legal means to do so.
- Communicating with a debtor or consumer by postcard.
- Using language that indicates you are a debt collector on the outside of an envelope sent to a debtor or consumer.
- Calling at a time you are aware is inconvenient for the debtor or consumer.
- Calling prior to 8 a.m. or after 9 p.m. at the debtor or consumers location.

HOW CAN YOU STAY UP TO DATE ON FDCPA UPDATES, CHANGES OR ADJUSTMENTS?

With debt collection in the news especially with all the negative publicity, rather than stories showing the positive affect the debt collection industry has on the economy and for businesses, it is imperative that you stay up to date on the FDCPA and any changes that may occur. Being a member of a credit industry association can help you stay up to date as well as reading the papers and keeping up to date on the news. Some important things to be aware of when collecting debts are the following:

Under what circumstances may a bill collector contact a debtors employer?

When trying to locate a debtor.

To enforce a judicial remedy.

When you have consent from the debtor.

Is it legal to mention legal action to a debtor on the phone or in a communication in writing involving a debt they are trying to collect?

Yes, a bill collector can mention legal action when trying to collect a debt ONLY if the collector can legally take that legal action and intends to take it. The FDCPA requires that if you state you will take legal action, you MUST have the authority to take that action. Be sure you have authority from your client to take any legal action you state you may take and also that the statute of limitations on the debt has not expired.

Can you tell a debtor that if they do not pay you will take "further action"?

Yes, but only if you have the authorization and capability to take further legal action. Use "further action" in the same context as "legal action".

Can you tell a debtor that their non-payment will affect their credit report?

Yes, but only if you can legally report the debt to the consumer reporting agency and intend to do so.

Can you tell a debtor that you will have them arrested if they do not make good on a bad check in a state where it is illegal to pass a bad check?

No, even in states where it is against the law to intentionally pass a bad check, not every bad check violates the law. Check the FDCPA , the laws in your state and remember that a bill collector cannot threaten to take any action that they cannot legally or don't intend to take. The bill collector cannot arrest a debtor, or be certain the authorities will arrest the debtor and so therefore cannot state they will be arrested.

What is the procedure a bill collector must take when they receive a written dispute from a debtor?

If you have already reported the debt to a credit bureau, you must notify that bureau that the debt is now disputed. If you receive the notification within the 30 days after the debtor has received notice of their rights to have the debt verified, you must cease collection of the debt until you can obtain and mail verification of the debt to the debtor. Take note that the verification must come from the bill collector, not your client. If the notice is received AFTER the 30 day period, the bill collector is under no obligation to verify the debt, though I believe it is a good business practice to do so.

How can a bill collector communicate with a debtor that has requested no further contact?

If you have received a notice from the debtor asking you to cease contact, or that they refuse to pay, you MUST cease all communications in relation to that specific debt EXCEPT to advise the consumer that you are terminating your collections efforts, or to notify the debtor that you or the creditor MAY take further action as allowed such as credit reporting or legal action. You must then follow through on those actions stated.

What to Watch for from Washington…

◆ More changes to the Fair Debt Collection Practices Act (FDCPA)

◆ More attempts to pass national privacy legislation

◆ Legislation that will give the FTC rule-making authority over the FDCPA

What to Watch for in your State…

◆ Regulations of medical collections

◆ Privacy and credit freeze statutes

◆ Stories about rogue collectors causing negative attention to the industry

CHAPTER THIRTEEN
COMPLIANCE PLANS

When dealing with compliance issues collection calls and letters should be your chief compliance concern. Otherwise you may find yourself being sued.

A compliance plan needs to:

◆ Set forth the principals outlining the policies of your agency
◆ Educate employees and/or train them on what happens when you do not comply with the compliance plan.

An effective compliance plan depends on each agency owner or worker fulfilling their duties and responsibilities with respect to their individual plan. An agency will be held accountable for failing to comply to the standard laws and procedures that are part of the plan. Remember as the agency owner, you are ultimately responsible for your employees actions, and must keep them educated and on track.

You need to keep up to date on any new laws or compliance issues and share that information with your employees. This is why it is a good idea to belong to industry credit groups or associations and to subscribe to at least one credit related magazine or newsletter.

The key parts of any compliance plan are:

PURPOSE

This provides standards for you and your employees that will protect and promote your agencies integrity and reputation.

INTRODUCTION

Your compliance program should consist of a code of conduct that applies to everyone at your agency. Some agencies appoint a Compliance Officer if they have a large staff. This person oversees development and serves as the one contact person for your employees to report any violations of your compliance program. If you have a very large agency, you may also consider having a Compliance Committee to help your Compliance Officer keep on top of these things. If you appoint a Compliance Officer, they need to:

- Develop, implement, educate and maintain the plan
- Review your plan as needed
- Have meetings or memos advising staff of new compliance or changes in compliance issues
- Educate staff on compliance
- Investigate reported violations
- Provide guidance and answers
- Keep compliance at the top of your list

RESOURCES FOR COMPLIANCE INFORMATION

Cornerstone Support Inc. – They can help collection agencies with compliance issues, and they assist agencies in obtaining licenses, bonds and foreign qualifications to be compliant wherever they collect. They are expensive but they do a good job. I dealt with Tony Bailey, email him at tony@cornerstonesupport.com.

Visit *www.collectionindustry.com* for articles, news and columns about compliance issues.

---

6 mistakes that can get you sued:

1. Not training employees with collection call training.

2. Not reviewing your collection letters.

3. Not correctly reporting to credit bureaus.

4. Not responding to "cease and desist" letters.

5. Not being educated about identity theft.

6. Not being properly licensed.

CHAPTER FOURTEEN
WHAT TO DO WITH A NEW ACCOUNT

You should have procedures in place on what to do when you receive a new account or client. This procedure should outline setting up a new client account or new debt collection account. This is especially important because of privacy laws, especially regarding the health care industry. To limit liability exposure, be sure to always send an acknowledgement to your clients when they place new accounts with you, either by email or postal mail. You can input all of the accounts and create a report or just print out the listing letting them know you have received and processed their accounts. Also, be sure to include the Mini-Miranda and validation notice on the first letter you send to the debtor and have an attorney check your debt collection letters to be sure you are in compliance. Make sure you back up your computer and keep very detailed notes with every contact you have with a debtor. Most collection software will automatically input the date and time of the call when you open a debtors account. Always get the name of who you spoke with and record the date, day and time of the call as well as what was said.

Your new client has placed some accounts with your agency for collection! Now what? Following are some steps you can take and make into a procedure for new accounts, or modify it to fit your agency or needs.

Step 1: Do a skip trace on the account if needed

Step 2: Input the account into your computer system

Step 3: Send out the Initial Collection Letter which includes the Mini Miranda

Step 4: Telephone call follow up, call after a few days, when the debtor should have received your letter.

Step 5: Take a payment over the phone or set up a payment plan or arrangement

Step 6: Follow up! Use your tickler file.

CHAPTER FIFTEEN
COLLECTION LETTERS

MINI MIRANDA

When you send your first collection letter to the debtor be sure to remember to include the mini Miranda, this is very important. You must include this by law. I have it listed here for you:

Unless you notify this office within 30 days after receiving this notice that you dispute the validity of this debt or any portion thereof, this office will assume this debt is valid. If you notify this office in writing within 30 days from receiving this notice, this office will: obtain verification of the debt or obtain a copy of a judgment and mail you a copy of such judgment or verification. If you request this office in writing within 30 days after receiving this notice, this office will provide you with the name and address of the original creditor, if different from the current creditor.

If you don't send a letter to the debtor before you make the first phone call be sure to say this in your initial phone call before you request payment on the debt.

For examples of dunning letters used by collection agencies, check out "The First book of Effective Collection Agency Letters & Forms" e-book at www.michelledunn.com ISBN# 0970664540 $19.95. You can use this book to create your own custom letters or use the ones included as they are. Remember, your letters should:

- Tell the reason for your letter (in the first sentence)
- Explain more about the reason for your letter (second sentence)
- Suggest a solution
- Thank the recipient

It is also a good idea to offer all payment options in your letter, such as credit or debit card options, or an addressed and sometimes postage paid envelope for a check or money order. Remember, the easier you make it for the debtor to make a payment, the better your chances of recovery.

CHAPTER SIXTEEN
THE FAIR CREDIT REPORTING ACT

REASONABLE PROCEDURES TO AVOID VIOLATIONS

Every consumer reporting agency must maintain reasonable procedures designed to avoid violations of Section 605 (obsolete information, reporting of voluntary closing of account, indication of dispute by consumer), and to limit the furnishing of consumer reports to the purposes listed under Section 604. "These procedures shall require that prospective users of the information identify themselves, certify the purposes for which the information is sought, and certify that the information will be used for no other purpose." See Section 607 of the Fair Credit Reporting Act, as amended.

VERIFY IDENTITY OF NEW PROSPECTIVE USER AND USES

"Every consumer reporting agency shall make a reasonable effort to verify the identity of a new prospective user and the uses certified by such prospective user prior to furnishing such user a consumer report. No consumer reporting agency may furnish a consumer report to any person if it has reasonable grounds for believing that the consumer report will not be used for a purpose listed in section 604 of this title."

The Fair Credit Reporting Act as amended by the Consumer Credit Reporting Reform Act of 1996, does not offer specific instruction on what actions constitute "reasonable effort." Some direction may be detected from the FTC Official Staff Commentary on the Fair Credit Reporting Act. Please note that this Commentary was written before the passage of the Consumer Credit Reporting Reform Act of 1996. Also note that the FTC "Commentary does not have the force of a statutory provision or trade regulation rule, and that it is not a binding ruling of any type." Always discuss actual cases with your actual attorney or legal department.

A PORTION OF SECTION 607 COMPLIANCE PROCEDURE

(a) Identity and purposes of credit users. Every consumer reporting agency shall maintain reasonable procedures designed to avoid violations of section 605 [§ 1681c] and to limit the furnishing of consumer reports to the purposes listed under section 604 [§ 1681b] of this title. These procedures shall require that prospective users of the information identify themselves, certify the purposes for which the information is sought, and certify that the information will be used for no other purpose. Every consumer reporting agency shall make a reasonable effort to verify the identity of a new prospective user and the uses certified by such prospective user prior to furnishing such user a consumer report. No consumer reporting agency may furnish a consumer report to any person if it has reasonable grounds for believing that the consumer report will not be used for a purpose listed in section 604 [§ 1681b] of this title.

CHAPTER SEVENTEEN

SKIP TRACING

WHAT IS SKIP TRACING?

Skip tracing is the process of tracking down someone who owes you money.

In order to successfully collect on a delinquent account, you have to locate the debtor. A debtor may relocate and/or have his telephone disconnected, believing they are leaving creditors with no immediate means of contact. There are many ways to try and find a debtor. Look in the local telephone book, or if they are in another state, or were in the past, you can use an online service.

A skip trace can be done for current address and phone, fictitious business names, social security death index, bankruptcies, judgments, liens, national property and deed transfers.

WHEN SHOULD YOU SKIP TRACE?

- When mail is returned
- When the phone is disconnected

SOME INFORMATION NEEDED FOR A PROFESSIONAL SKIP TRACE

- Full Name (first, middle, last)
- Social Security Number
- Date of Birth
- Former Address
- Employment Information
- Vehicle and Drivers License Information
- Spouse Information

To get started with skip tracing you need to know where to go to look for and find your debtors. You need to get all the information together that you have on the debtor.

FINDING DEBTORS

There are many ways to try to find a debtor. Look in a local telephone book, or if they are in another state, or were in the past, you can use an online service such as www.555-1212.com or www.411locate.com. You can also call directory assistance if you have an idea in which town the debtor might be located.

You can pull a credit report on the debtor. You may find a wealth of information here! It could list the last known address and employment, or if they own property and/or a vehicle. You can also call any creditors that are listed on the credit report and ask if they have an address for your debtor.

Other places you can check by going to your local courthouse or town hall in some cases:

- ◆ Traffic records
- ◆ Circuit civil records
- ◆ County civil records
- ◆ Circuit criminal records
- ◆ County criminal records
- ◆ Voter registration
- ◆ Marriage records
- ◆ Occupational license
- ◆ Property tax rolls
- ◆ Hunting and fishing licenses
- ◆ Property records
- ◆ Automobile registration

You can search online for a debtor using various methods. Search by name, phone number, address, state or email address. You can do reverse lookups and more. Some sites offer this service free, other charge a fee. I have had better luck with fee-based services. We have a large listing of free and fee based skip tracing tools at www.credit-and-collections.com under "Resources." Here are some of the places you can try:

FREE LOOKUPS

- 411 Locate - www.411locate.com
- 411 Locate in Canada -canada411.sympatico.ca
- Free Email address directory -www.emailaddresses.com
- Telephone Directories on the Web -www.teldir.com/eng
- The Ultimate Yellow Pages -www.theultimates.com/yellow
- Worldpages Phone Search -www.worldpages.com
- Search systems.net

FEE BASED SKIP TRACING

- Flat Rate Info.com www.flatrateinfo.com
- Search America www.searchamerica.com
- Accurint www.accurint.com
- US Tracers, Inc. www.ustracers.com
- VeriFacts, Inc. 815-380-9614 ask for Jodi Matteson

You also need to decide how you want to be paid for skip tracing. Some agencies include this in their collection commission. Others offer it as a special service and charge a flat rate or an hourly rate. You might want to surf the web and see what other agencies are charging.

Top 8 tips for finding a debtor

1.   Make sure you don't lie and pretend you are looking for someone for a different reason than what you do.

2.   Make note of all information gathered from a credit report. Keep note of age, marital status, type of employment, interests, this can all help you investigate and find your debtor.

3.   Utilize public records. Hunting and fishing licenses and dog licensing are often overlooked.

4.   Utilize your courthouse or their website for public records.

5.   Visit the library and look through yearbooks.

6.   Look through obituaries for relatives.

7.   Are they divorced? Ex's are sometimes happy to give you information.

8.   Leave basic messages, just your name, phone number and a reference number (not account number), this causes curiosity and can get your call returned.

CHAPTER EIGHTEEN

HEALTH CARE COLLECTIONS

Physicians of all types as well as hospitals are dealing with more and more bad debt, and trying to figure out how to utilize collection agencies to help them recover some of their money. According to research done by Kaulkin Ginsberg, the 6000 hospitals in the United States generate roughly $129 billion in bad debt a year and $42.6 billion of that is placed or sold each year. The expectation in the coming years is that people will be paying 30% of their hospital bills, today it is less than 5%. Hospitals struggle to collect from patients, so this is a good specialized area for collection agencies to target.

Most hospitals in the U.S. write off balances to bad debt after 180 days, which is when they place the accounts with a collection agency. Some hospitals do not even want to place those accounts with an agency but would rather sell the debt. Some agencies consider purchasing debt in addition to offering a contingency option.

Collection agencies that want to specialize or participate in doing health care recovery must align their strategies with the hospitals credit department or collection parameters. They need to keep a close eye on customer complaints and the increasing state and federal regulations in relation to health care collections. Hospitals traditionally rely on third party or insurance companies to pay 90% of their payments. Normally they will try to collect the other 10% from the patient and if they don't have luck after approximately 180 days they will write the balance off to bad debt. Then they may sell the debt or place it with an agency.

Hospitals, doctors, emergency rooms and clinics are all very concerned with customer service, which might explain their reluctance to utilize a collection agency. If you decide to do healthcare collections, keep in mind that you may need to brush up on your customer service skills. Many of the accounts you will be trying to collect on will be local people, keep this in mind when making calls and sending letters.

Most hospitals and clinics will continue to do business with the people you are trying to collect from.

To win a health care provider's business a collection agency must be willing to put customer service at the top of its benefits or priority list. Your reputation as a considerate, law abiding agency will be very important to this type of client. Also keep in mind that many times you will end up dealing with an insurance company rather than the patient or debtor.

Number of U.S. Hospitals	6,000
Healthcare Revenues	$202 trillion
Average amount of bad debt written-off by hospitals	$15 million
Percentage that is written off	6.4%
Amount of bad debt in the healthcare industry	$129 billion
Amount of bad debt placed or sold	$426 billion (33%)
Average recovery rate	25%
Gross Recoveries for healthcare providers	$10.6 billion
Average contingency fee for healthcare placements	23%
Source: Kaulkin Ginsberg	

CHAPTER NINETEEN
PRESS RELEASES

HOW DO YOU KNOW WHEN TO WRITE A PRESS RELEASE?

Writing press releases, or having someone write them for you, is very important to your business. You want all the free publicity you can get!

The times to write a press release are:
- When you open your collection agency
- When you or your agency wins an award
- When you develop a new service
- When you launch a new program or website
- When you hire new employees

The best way to send press releases is to fax or email them to the newspaper office. Look in your local phone book for the newspapers in your area. Call and ask for the fax number and the name of the person to whom you should address press releases, or you can look online if they have a website.

Don't get discouraged if they don't print them right away. I probably sent 20 press releases before one was published!

When should you send press releases?
- When you open your agency
- When you or your agency wins an award or receives recognition for something
- When you create a website
- When you offer a new service
- When you have your one year, 2 year, 3 year anniversary etc.
- When you expand, hire new employees or move
- When you join an organization such as your local Chamber, Credit & Collections or any other association
- When you give to charity or help someone for free

TIP: Visit www.credit-and-collections.com and join today, then send out this press release. Also, email michelle@credit-and-collections.com if your release is published and Michelle will put it in the next issue of the Become the Squeaky Wheel. *Free publicity for you!*

Here is a press release I wrote and sent out when my agency had been in business for 5 years. Example of Press release #1:

FOR IMMEDIATE RELEASE

For Additional information:
Michelle A Dunn
Collection Agency
Phone number

COLLECTION AGENCY CELEBRATES 5 YEARS IN BUSINESS!

Plymouth – *Collection Agency,* a leader in the Collection Industry, celebrated its 5-year anniversary in January. Company president, Michelle Dunn, said, "In the 'new economy' a business that stays around for more than a year is news. In the 'old economy' it is said that 80% of businesses fail within their first 5 years of operation. New economy, old economy, or whatever economy you want to talk about, successfully being in business for 5 years is something to be proud of.

Michelle Dunn started *Collection Agency* in January 1998. Since it was started, there have been many changes. *Collection Agency* offers collection services; skip tracing services, Accounts Receivable outsourcing and more for its clients. *Collection Agency* offers online account placement, online payment options and lots of FREE information for people in business, such as free credit applications, and collection letters. There is also a free e-book available for download to anyone who visits the MAD site, with helpful Credit and Collection forms and letters.

Michelle has also written a book on How to Start your own Collection Agency, which is available on www.michelledunn.com and www.credit-and-collections.com. Michelle is also in the process of writing a third book for any business owner or anyone who works in credit or accounts receivable on how to create a credit policy in house to avoid bad debt problems.

Collection Agency is a full service collection agency. For more information on any of *Collection Agency's* services, visit the website at www.michelledunn.com or email Michelle at michelle@credit-and-collections.com

Press release example #2:

FOR IMMEDIATE RELEASE

For Additional information:
  Michelle A Dunn
  Collection Agency
  Phone number

Collection Agency launches Free Online Credit and Collections Community

Holderness NH – Michelle Dunn, owner of *Collection Agency*, has launched an online credit and collections community. This online community has an email discussion list for business people in the credit and collections field. "We share ideas, information, and stories. It's a great opportunity to Network", says Dunn.

This list is for small and large business owners, entrepreneurs and anyone in the credit & collections field. There is also a website for all members where they can get free advertising for their business by adding a link to their website.

The website www.credit-and-collections.com offers other ways to advertise your site for free; articles can be submitted with a free link to your site or email address. There are many resources for business owners, or credit managers that need ideas or help in getting their receivables under control. The Fair Debt Collection Practices Act is also highlighted. There is also a bookstore with books about collecting debt, taking someone to small claims court and collection laws.

Anyone and everyone is welcome to join or just to visit the website for free information to help you in collecting money from your customers.

For more information on any of Michelle's Collection Agency services, visit the website at www.credit-and-collections.com or email Michelle at michelle@credit-and-collections.com

Press release example #3:

FOR IMMEDIATE RELEASE

12/1/00

Michelle A Dunn

603-536-0000

Collection Agency offers online bill paying

Holderness – *Collection Agency* has a new service on its website, where you can pay your debt online at www.credit-and-collections.com. "A lot of debtors want to pay their bill without having to call or make out a check", says Dunn, owner of *Collection Agency.* "This way they can go online and pay with Pay pal, check online or check by fax and coming soon by credit card." Clients can also use the online forms to pay an invoice or for a skip trace service they need.

Collection Agency already has an online "placement of accounts" form where clients can place accounts online at their leisure. "It is convenient and they can do it anytime, day or night" says Dunn. "Most accounts that are placed with us are now placed through our online forms."

For more information on placing accounts or paying a bill online visit Michelle's websites at www.michelledunn.com or www.credit-and-collections.com or email Michelle at michelle@credit-and-collections.com

Places to post your press releases for FREE online

www.prweb.com/

www.powerhomebiz.com/biznews/pressrelease.htm

www.addpr.com/addrelease.php

www.24-7pressrelease.com/

http://press.heliographica.com

www.free-press-release.com

www.prfree.com

www.pressmethod.com

www.press-base.com

www.click2newsites.com/press.asp

www.clickpress.com

www.pressbox.co.uk

www.cadenasmarketing.com

http://news.eboomwebsolutions.com/addnews.php

www.i-newswire.com/submit_free.php

http://press.arrivenet.com/

www.prleap.com

www.webnewswire.com/submit.html

www.webwire.com/

More places to post your press releases for FREE online

www.michelledunn.com

www.articleresponder.com

www.echievements.com

www.success.com/newsletters.php

www.homehighlight.org

www.netterweb.com

www.thewebcontent.com

www.morganarticlearchive.com

http://ezinearticles.com/

http://goarticles.com/

www.creditguru.com

www.freesticky.com

www.howtoadvice.com

www.sohoday.com

http://searchwarp.com

www.articlemarketer.com

http://killermarketingarsenal.com

http://articlehub.com/add.html

www.boomercafe.com/guidelines.htm

www.content-articles.com

CHAPTER TWENTY
PERSONNEL

Even if you are not looking for personnel as you start your agency you will want to make sure you have the necessary knowledge and skills to be a good collector and business owner. To do well in this business you need to have good communication skills, listening skills, negotiation or mediation skills and organizational skills. You need to be able to persuade business owners to hire you as their collection service when their outstanding accounts are still new and you need to convince the debtors you contact to send you money. You should have a clear knowledge of credit management and credit policies.

Patience is a huge part of being a bill collector, in order to stay in control of a situation, a phone call or a payment plan you must have patience. You must be firm but fair with the people you are calling.

You can also never stop learning, make sure you are up to date on the FDCPA and the FCRA as well as any changes that can affect how you do business. If you will be collecting on medical bills you need to have an understanding of health insurance policies and billing practices and you must learn about HIPAA the Health Insurance Portability and Accountability Act of 1996. This Act addresses the security and privacy of health data and information.

As a bill collector and agency owner you will deal with all kinds of people in different situations. Being an entrepreneur and business owner is a tough job and being a bill collector and agency owner is even more challenging.

When you find you need to hire some help for your agency, whether it is a receptionist, secretary or a collector it is crucial to hire the right people. Asking the right questions during the interview process is important. Some questions you may want to consider are:
Why do you want to work here?
Why are you changing jobs?
What do you think you could improve on in your current job?
What can you tell me about the company you work for?

What can you tell me about my company?
What's the most interesting job you have had?
Why did you leave that job?
What do you like best about your current job?

You might also want to ask them about their current job duties, for example how many credit applications do they process per day, what is the criteria for approving or denying credit, how do they handle credit and collection disputes.

Once you hire someone to work at your agency, remember what a tough job it is. Collection agencies and credit departments have a high turnover rate because of the nature of the job. Once you find and train your staff you want to keep them, give them reasons to stay working at your agency. Always remember to tell them when they do a good job, maybe make a small gesture such as buying them coffee or lunch as a reward for a job well done. You could also offer a bonus or gift certificate. Remember the importance of saying thank you. You don't even have to spend any extra money, but being appreciative and understanding goes a long way.

When you first start your agency you will probably do everything yourself. This will include making phone calls, selling accounts, mailing letters, recruiting clients, doing the bookkeeping, handling disputes, and more. As you get clients and more accounts you may need to hire help. Tasks such as marketing your business and bookkeeping take away from collecting. If you hire someone to do the collection work, you need to be prepared to hire an experienced collector, or be willing to educate him or her on proper collection techniques. Employees need to know all the laws in the states they will be collecting, and what they can and cannot do by law and in accordance with the FDCPA. Some of the qualities you may look for when looking for someone to help you with collecting are reasoning skills, patience, communication skills, and great follow-up skills. Sometimes all the collector is to the debtor is a mediator. You may also need to train someone to do skip tracing, or train them in locating debtors that have skipped town.

The salary you pay your collectors will vary based on experience and your region of the country. Some agencies pay a low salary and give a commission based on what is collected. Check out what collectors are being paid in your general area to get an idea. Remember, your employee is not you. You need to compromise and be satisfied, as long as they are doing what they are expected to do.

Develop a job description, training, flip charts, or tip/cheat sheets for your collectors. You can find information on flip charts, cheat sheets and training at www.michelledunn.com or www.credit-and-collections.com

Will you need a collector who is bilingual? Make sure you have job applications and check references, and also do a credit check if you are set up to pull credit reports. There are certain things you can and can't ask a potential employee.

CAN ASK	CAN'T ASK
Verify age	What is your age
Convicted of any felonies	Marital status
Sexual preference	Do you have children under 18

How will you decide how much to pay your collectors? Check out what others are paying their collectors and check the job history of the applicants to see what their pay was at their last job. You can also contact a company such as Accountemps, www.accountemps.com, (800) 803-8367 for more information. I have provided a salary guide for you below. Remember this is just a guide and is based on research I have done as of the printing of this book.

Large companies

Credit Manager	$55,000 - $76,000
Assistant Credit Manager	$43,000 - $57,500
Credit Analyst	$34,500 - $45,550

Credit/Collections Clerk	$29,000 - $35,550
Medium companies	
Credit Manager	$45,200 - $57,200
Assistant Credit Manager	$36,500 - $45,250
Credit/Collections Clerk	$25,800 – $32,000
Small companies	
Credit Manager	$37,200 - $49,000
Assistant Credit Manager	$31,250 - $39,000
Credit/Collections Clerk	$24,500 - $30,000

Some agencies offer a commission on monies collected in addition to an hourly wage or a salary. At some agencies collectors must have $3,000.00 in commission on the board before they start collecting commission for themselves. This pays for the agencies overhead and their salary. Once they hit their plateau of $3,000.00 - they get 25% of all commission they bring in.

When writing your job description, remember that it has to establish the framework for defining the job, will give the potential employee a clear idea of what to expect and what is expected of them, serves as a tool when doing performance reviews. Your job descriptions should include:

- Position title
- General description of duties
- Key responsibilities
- Skills needed to perform the job
- Educational requirements

Below is a Job Description you can use for a collector. Remember that you can customize this to fit your agency. Also, you would want to be more specific in some areas, such as under computer skills, you should indicate what software you use and if you want the collector to be experienced in this or if you will train.

DEBT COLLECTOR JOB DESCRIPTION

Job title: Debt collector

Description:

- To maintain, track and collect on 250 accounts.
- To provide quarterly reports
- To ensure compliance with all State & Federal laws
- To read, interpret and apply laws, rules, regulations, policies and/or procedures
- To make a decision or solve a problem by using logic, identify key facts, explore alternatives, and propose quality solutions

Required skills:

- Computer skills
- Knowledge of Credit Management
- Skip tracing knowledge
- Mediation skills
- Negotiation skills
- Communication skills
- Patience
- Good follow up skills

Duties & Responsibilities:

- Debt collection of accounts by phone and mail.
- Attendance of credit meetings and seminars.
- Some Field Collections
- Full knowledge of the FDCPA & FCRA
- Some court appearances
- Research disputes
- Provide documentation to support debts
- Other Requirements

This job will be done while sitting but there may be some walking; standing; bending; carrying of light items such as papers or books; or driving an automobile. No special physical demands are required to perform the work.

Being a debt collector is a hard job. Sometimes it is discouraging and collectors can be cranky and unhappy if they have to deal with rude or loud debtors. Being hung up on and called names can also take its toll. Some ways you can help keep your collectors happy are:

Loosen up – allow some mistakes to happen, as long as they are not violations of the law, and take steps to help prevent them in the future. Use each mistake as a learning experience for everyone.

Recognize your collectors as often as possible. Just a thank you, or buying someone a cup of coffee to thank them for a job well done, is a big boost to morale.

Teach your collectors. Boss's who teach and help others are much better received than someone who is barking orders all the time.

Sometimes you may just need a part time helper, this can be a teenager or intern from your local college. I have had many part time people help me with my agency, including my children. Some of the tasks I had them do were:
- Fold letters (until I purchased a letter folding machine)
- Stuff envelopes
- Run mail through the postage meter
- Take mail to the post office and get mail trays as needed
- When I hired someone with more experience I had them do all of the above and also added:
- Skip tracing
- File backup
- Handling bankruptcy notices
- Sending backup documentation out to debtors
- Answering the phone (be sure to tell them to sound happy!)

You may also want to hire an office manager. I hired an office manager and trained her on the FDCPA and had her listen to me make calls, and then gradually introduced her to making collection calls or answering the phone and being able to help the debtor who was calling in. Here is an example of my office managers job description:

OFFICE MANAGER JOB DESCRIPTION

- Check voice mail and handle messages, return calls or pass on messages
- Prepare outgoing mail
- Filing
- Make collection calls
- Input accounts

Then when I wrote and was selling my books I added keeping track of book orders, and also skip trace orders. You can also have your office manager, clean your office, and do anything that will free up your time to make more collection calls. You can purchase Applications for Employment at an office supply store, download them online or create your own. Be sure to include the following statement:

It is our policy to provide equal employment opportunity to all qualified persons without regard to race, creed, color, religious belief, sex, age, national origin, ancestry, physical or mental handicap or veteran status.

And also at the bottom where the applicant signs the application, include something like:

I certify that the facts set forth in this application for employment are true and complete to the best of my knowledge. I understand that if I am employed, false statements on this application shall be considered sufficient cause for my dismissal. This company is hereby authorized to make any investigations of my prior educational and employment history. I understand that employment at this company is "at will", which means that either I or this company can terminate this employment relationship at any time, with or without prior notice.

Be sure the applicant signs the application and check all references and pull a credit report if possible.

CHAPTER TWENTY-ONE
BUYING DEBT

If you decide to purchase debt to collect for your agency, you need to be aware of some other laws. Some states subject debt buyers to collection statutes and some do not. Some states do not really have very clear laws on this type of situation. We have listed them here for you.

You can purchase debt online or through many different resellers. One that I have used is "Charge Off Clearing House." You can check out their site at www.chargeoffclearinghouse.com. The good thing about buying debt is you can get it fairly inexpensively, and you keep all that you collect!

Tips when buying debt, check to see how many other agencies may have worked the accounts, are the deceased and bankruptcy accounts removed? How old are the accounts? Will you have to skip trace? Has the debt been reported to the credit bureaus? Check out www.collectionindustry.com and www.chargeoffclearinghouse.com for more information and articles that can help you decide if buying debt is right for you. When you contact Charge off Clearing house, ask for Louise Epstein, she is a great lady who can help you even if you have never bought debt before and have no idea what you are looking for. She buys & sells receivables, provides expert witness and consulting services to qualified issuers and debt buying firms.

Please visit your state's website for more information:

Alabama	www.alabama.gov
Alaska	www.state.ak.us
Arizona	www.az.gov
California	www.ca.gov/state
Colorado	www.colorado.gov/
Connecticut	www.ct.gov/
Delaware	www.delaware.gov/
Florida	www.myflorida.com
Georgia	www.georgia.gov
Hawaii	www.ehawaiigov.org/
Idaho	www.accessidaho.org/
Illinois	www.illinois.gov/
Indiana	www.state.in.us/
Iowa	www.state.ia.us/
Kansas	www.accesskansas.org/
Kentucky	www.ky.gov
Louisiana	www.state.la.us/
Maine	www.state.me.us/
Maryland	www.maryland.gov/
Michigan	www.michigan.gov/
Minnesota	www.governor.state.mn.us/
Mississippi	www.mississippi.gov/
Missouri	www.state.mo.us/
Montana	www.state.mt.us
Nebraska	www.nebraska.gov
Nevada	www.nv.gov/
New Hampshire	www.state.nh.us/
New Jersey	www.state.nj.us/
New Mexico	www.state.nm.us/
New York	www.state.ny.us/
North Carolina	www.ncgov.com/
North Dakota	http://discovernd.com/
Ohio	www.state.oh.us/
Oklahoma	www.youroklahoma.com/
Rhode Island	www.state.ri.us/

South Carolina	www.myscgov.com
South Dakota	www.state.sd.us/
Tennessee	www.state.tn.us/
Texas	www.state.tx.us/
Utah	www.utah.gov/
Vermont	http://vermont.gov/

CHAPTER TWENTY-TWO
RESOURCES

CREDIT

- Affiliate or Franchise Collection Agency - www.national1credit.com/Franchise.html or Email David at satellite@national1credit.com or call him at 212-679-2007 and tell him Michelle Dunn sent you.
- Equifax - www.Equifax.com
- Experian - www.experian.com
- Federal Trade Commisison - www.ftc.gov
- Trans Union - www.tuc.com
- Credit and Collections - www.credit-and-collections.com
- Creditworthy Co. - www.creditworthy.com
- Credit Risk Monitor - www.creditriskmonitor.com
- Eli Research - www.eliresearch.com
- Kaulkin Media, Collection Industry.com - www.collectionindustry.com
- Business Info Guide.com - www.businessinfoguide.com
- International Association of Commercial Collectors, President: David Ward www.commercialcollector.com
- Credit Tools, News & Reference www.cardreport.com
- Helpful legal resources www.FindLaw.com

COLLECTION JOB REFERRALS

- www.collectionindustry.com/jobs/

SKIP TRACING

- 555-1212 - www.555-1212.com
- Flat Rate Info.com - www.flatrateinfo.com
- 411 Locate - www.411locate.com/body.htm
- Telephone directories on the web - www.teldir.com/eng

- Skip Trace Combo Pack – www.rcinfoservices.com
- Switchboard - www.switchboard.com
- Corporate information - www.corporateinformation.com
- Pacific Information Resources Inc. DBA Search Systems - www.searchsystems.net
- Insight America - www.insightamerica.com
- DataServ - www.dataserv.info Email Larry Borsi at lborsi@voltdelta.com
- Search America - www.searchamerica.com 763-416-1040 ask for John Moroz
- Universal Communications - www.uccweb.com Ask for or email Jim Stegner
- American Research Bureau Inc. - www.arbi.com Email Todd Landing at Toddlansing@arbi.com
- VeriFacts Inc., 815-380-9614, Ask for Jodi Matteson.
- US Tracers, Inc. - www.ustracers.com or call 800-360-5601
- IM411 - www.im411.com or call 800-308-1007
- Real EDA Information Services, Network Dimensions Inc. - www.RealEDA.com or call 908-876-5549 and ask for Gary Christopher
- Locate Plus - www.locateplus.com
- American Research Bureau (reasonably priced, no-prepayments or applications) - www.arbi.com

NETWORKING
- Credit and Collections - www.credit-and-collections.com
- Creditworthy.com - www.creditworthy.com
- Digital Women - www.digital-women.com
- Entrepreneurial Edge Online - www.edgeonline.com
- Women Inspiring women – www.wiwnh.com

STARTING YOUR BUSINESS
- Small business association - www.sba.gov
- Quicken - www.quicken.com

- Business Resource Center - www.morebuisness.com
- Anything and Everything Business - www.allbusiness.com
- Glover Enterprise - www.gloverenterprise.com
- Another8Hours - www.Another8Hours.com
- WoW! Graphic Designs - www.wowgraphicdesigns.com
- Michelle Dunn Online – www.michelledunn.com
- Admin Solutions - www.admin-solutions.com
- Triple J WordProcessing Co. - www.triple-j.net
- All Business – www.allbusiness.com

TAXES AND ACCOUNTING
- Nicholson Tax & Accounting - www.nicholsontaxandaccounting.com, Ask for Diane.

LICENSES & PERMITS
- www.irs.gov/
- www.sba.gov/
- www.firstgov.gov

CHILD SUPPORT COLLECTIONS
- www.childsupportoptions.org
- www.supportguidelines.com/links.html

PURCHASING DEBT
- Charge off Clearinghouse - www.chargeoffclearinghouse.com. Louise Epstein, President 512-502-0300

BUSINESS SERVICES
- ADH Administrative Services - www.adhadmin.com
- Provides mail & e-mail services, small business marketing, secretarial services and more. Contact Toni Henry at 630-208-0138 for a free one-hour consultation!
- My Business Connection - http://mybusinessconnection.net Call Kim Beasley 404-506-9351. She provides simple business solutions.
- Your Virtual Personal Assistant, Sharon Trombly "Business growth without staff expenses" www.tromblycommunications.com

- Virtual Gal Friday – Every Company's Administrative Assistant - www.virtualgalfriday.com, Ask for Nancy Brown.
- Administrative Support Services - www.healershelper.com Ask for Rita Ballard

WEBSITE HOSTING

- WoW! Graphic Designs - www.wowgraphicdesigns.com Ask for Cheryl Microutsicos.
- A World of Difference in web design - www.msdetta.com Ask for Diane Hildebrandt.
- Michelle Bailey - www.shoppingalacart.com
- Sphynx Consulting Group - www.sphynxconsulting.com Ask for Joy Byers.
- Hosting Connecticut LLC - http://hostingct.com Ask for Paula Peirce.

MERCHANT ACCOUNTS FOR COLLECTION AGENCIES

- Jason Chacon, Payments Team, www.usaepp.com
- Electronic Payment Providers, Inc., 2999 N. 44th Street Suite #415, Phoenix, AZ 85018, (877) EPP-CORP, (602) 667-9565 Ext. 206
- National Payments, Inc. – Call 949.722.7755 or email Peter D, Hoyt at peter.hoyt@nationalpayments.com

STARTING A COLLECTION AGENCY CONSULTING

- Michelle Dunn Online & Credit & Collections.com - www.michelledunn.com/resources/consulting-collection-agency.html
- Tim Paulsen - www.trpaulsen.com

PUBLIC RELATIONS

- Women's News Bureau, Call 770-603-6521 or visit www.womensnewsbureau.com

RECOMMENDED READING

The First Book of Effective Collection Agency Letters & Forms by Michelle Dunn. ISBN# 0970664540 Available as an e-book at www.michelledunn.com $19.95

Become the Squeaky Wheel, a Credit & Collections Guide for Everyone by Michelle Dunn ISBN# 0970664516 Available for $29.99 e-book or paperback copy from www.michelledunn.com www.amazon.com or your local bookstore.

Authors Note* I have had many collection agencies purchase bulk copies of this book to give their clients as a "Thank you" for doing business with them. They do this to educate their clients and make their job easier. So if you want to make more money with less effort, contact me about bulk orders at michelle@michelledunn.com with Bulk orders in the subject line.

The Fair Debt Collection Practices Act, U.S. Code Anotated. St. Paul, MN: West Publishing Company, updated annually and available in libraries.

Manhunt: The Book, by Joseph Culligan, Harvey Alters, Millard Land and Ron Brown.

How to Negotiate Like a Pro, 41 rules for resolving disputes by Mary Greenwood, J.D., LL.M

COLLECTION MAGAZINES

Collection Advisor Magazine, Contact T. Allen Rose, CPA, Editor/ Publisher, cpa@cpamag.com and www.collectionadvisor.com

Collections & Credit Risk monthly magazine: www.mediaowners.com/company/thomson.html. They also offer many other FREE Trade publications.

The Authority for Commercial and Consumer Credit Professionals, and they also offer CCR Newsline which is a twice weekly summary of News for Commercial and Consumer Credit Professionals. Visit www.creditcollectionsworld.com/ to subscribe to either one.

Credit Collections & Risk, Contact Stephen Kiely, email him at stephenjjkiely@gmail.com

Business Credit Magazine if you are a member of the NACM, 8840 Columbia 100 Parkway, Columbia, MD 21045-2158

NCN, National Credit News www.ncnjournal.com

SOFTWARE

- ◆ Collect! For Windows - Contact Greg Strong, Account Manager, Comtech Systems Inc. Phone: 250.391.0466 www.collect.org
- ◆ Abacus Totality www.totalitysoftware.com Ask for Evan Zucker
- ◆ At Point, Inc. Debt Collection Software Solution http://www.atpoint.com/products.html Email George A. Gyure at george@atpoint.com and tell him Michelle Dunn sent you. At Point Inc. has used the following forms that Michelle Dunn specially provided for use in their product:
  – Collection agreement
  – Interest letter
  – Proposal letter
  – Request for payment
  – Thank you letter

FREE Resources to help you start and grow your agency or business

How to Make Money Collecting Money, by Michelle Dunn. FREE E-book, if you are thinking about or are starting a collection agency.

Download my free e-book to help answer your questions as you start out. When you download this valuable free e-book you will learn about what collection agencies do and if you can start your own agency. You'll also receive examples of forms, letters and documents you can use when setting up your agency, helpful links and resources and a list of *Frequently Asked Questions*. Visit www.michelledunn.com/free.html to get your free copy today.

Free Newsletter, *The Collection Connection*, Subscribe for free at www.credit-and-collections.com/members.html

Free Newsletter, *Agency News*, subscribe at www.collectionindustry.com, A monthly newsletter with news and articles of interest to collection agency professionals.

Also see the chapter in this book on PRESS RELEASES for a listing of FREE places to post press releases and articles about your business to generate free publicity.

CCR Newsline a collections & credit risk news service - www.creditcollectionsworld.com/ccnsub.htm

Be sure to tell them Michelle Dunn sent you.

CHAPTER TWENTY-THREE
BAD CHECKS

Bad check information (subject to change without notice)

PLEASE NOTE Bad check laws do not apply when an individual stops payment on a check UNLESS it can be proven that the issuer of the check intended to stop the check when he presented the check for payment. Some states authorize the receiver of a bad check to collect a service charge to compensate for bank fees and/or cost incurred as a result of receiving and collecting on a bad check.

Following is a list of approved fees that can be collected on a returned check in each state: Contract with consumer.

ALABAMA	$27
ALASKA	$25
ARIZONA	$25
ARKANSAS	$20
CALIFORNIA	$25 for first check and a service fee of up to $35 for each subsequent check to the same payee
COLORADO	$20
FLORIDA	$25 if face value does not exceed $50, $30 if the face value exceeds $50 but does not exceed $300, $40 if the face value exceeds $300 or 5% of the face value of the check, which ever is greater.
GEORGIA	$25 or 5% of check, whichever is greater, to be paid in 10 days.
HAWAII	$20
IDAHO	$20, notice must have been given at time of sale
ILLINOIS	$25 OR all costs & expenses.
INDIANA	$20 or 5% of check, whichever is greater, not to exceed $250, due in 10 days.
IOWA	$20 posted conspicuously or 5% of the face, which ever is greater. $50 if the check is presented twice
KANSAS	$10 due in 14 days

LOUISIANA	$25 or 5% of face amount, whichever is greater, posted at point of sale
MAINE	Through civil action only, not to exceed $50 or an amount agreed in contract with consumer
MARYLAND	$25
MICHIGAN	$25 to be paid within 7 days, if not paid as requested, but within 30 days the service fee is $35
MINNESOTA	$20 posted at point-of-sale OR actual cost of collection not to exceed $30
MISSISSIPPI	$30 with payment to be made within 15 days
MISSOURI	$20
MONTANA	$30
NEVADA	$25
NEW HAMPSHIRE	$25 or an amount agreed to in contract with consumer
NEW YORK	$20
NORTH CAROLINA	$25
NORTH DAKOTA	$20
OHIO	$30 or 10% of face value of check, whichever is greater
OREGON	$25
PENNSYLVANIA	$20 if notice prominently displayed at point of sale, when check is issued and after conviction
RHODE ISLAND	$25 after 30 days
SOUTH CAROLINA	$25 or $30 for checks over $100
SOUTH DAKOTA	$30
TENNESSEE	an amount up to $20
TEXAS	$25 plus sales tax
UTAH	$20
VIRGINIA	$25
WASHINGTON	fee not to exceed $40 or face value of check, plus interest of 12% per annum as long as check is not for payment of interest, collection costs or attorneys fees
WEST VIRGINIA	$15
WISCONSIN	reasonable collection costs
WYOMING	$30

CHAPTER TWENTY-FOUR
DEFINITIONS USED IN CREDIT AND COLLECTIONS

BANKRUPT: insolvent, gone belly up, ruined, wiped out, broke, busted, penniless, in the red.

COLLECT: Accumulate or assemble, gather, harvest, reap, amass, hoard, save, round up, pile up, squirrel away, compile, congregate, flock, group, muster, convene, meet, cluster.

COLLECTION: Accumulation, mass, group, assortment, assembly, pile, gathering, stockpile, store, hoard, cluster, congregation, aggregation, compilation, anthology, hodgepodge.

CREDIT: Belief, trust, faith, honesty, credibility, praise, attribute, notice, commendation, debt on account, deferred payment, charge, time, installment plan.

DEBT: Obligation, liability, bill, debit, arrears, deficit, pledge, due, burden, red ink.

DEFAULT: Shirk, welsh, fail, stiff, skip out, run out on, dodge.

MONEY: Currency, legal tender, cash, bucks, dough, bread, medium of exchange, was, loot, scratch, wampum, coin, specie, tal, riches.

PAY: Remit, compensate, disburse, settle, cough up, foot the bill, spend, expend, shell out, fork over, pick up the tab, contribute, bankroll, finance.

SKIP: Hop, spring, leap, caper, romp, jump, cavort, gambol, prance, frisk, bounce, overlook, pass over, omit, exclude, leave out, forget about, disregard, never mind, ignore.

CREDITOR: Person who offers or extends credit creating a debt.

DEBT COLLECTOR: Any person, other than the creditor who regularly collects debts for others.

DEBTOR: Any person obligated or allegedly obligated to pay a debt.

DUN & BRADSTREET: An agency that furnishes subscribers with market statistics and credit ratings of businesses.

REPARATION: paying back, making amends; compensation

MEDIATION: an attempt by parties to resolve disputes with the aid of a facilitator.

DUNNING: the name used for notices sent out to collect money owed

FORWARDING: Term used when you forward or send an account to another agency to collect on.

CHAPTER TWENTY-FIVE
BUILDING A WEBSITE FOR YOUR AGENCY

Building a website does not have to be expensive I started out by using a free web site creator at Angelfire.com, until I had enough money and clients to buy my own domain name and hosting space. You can do the same at Angelfire, Geo Cities and many more.

Once you can afford to get your own domain name, visit www.networksolutions.com to sign up with a domain name you want. There may be other places to get a domain name but this is the one that I use. You will then need to host your website. There are many web hosting companies around. I use www.wowgraphicdesigns.com, this is owned by my good friend Cheryl, who is very helpful, professional and affordable. I have been using her services for almost 10 years now and have never had any problems. When you have a question, she will answer your call or email right away and do whatever it takes to get you where you want to be. Your hosting company can often provide domain registration and consolidated billing for your domain name, so that you only have one company you have to interact with. They will also set up your email addresses with your URL extension.

Once you have your URL and it is hosted you will need to create a website or hire someone to do it for you. I did my own at first but then became very busy and had to hire someone. If you do your own, you will need an FTP program to upload your work to the website. If you have time to do this yourself, it will save you a lot of money.

Remember that just having a website does not mean people can find it. You will need to promote your website online and off. You should print your URL on everything, letterhead, business cards, promotional items and brochures. Also, having a website means having a 24 hour storefront that is open, people from all over the world can check out what you have to offer any time of the day or night. If you have online services this will drive more traffic to your site. Some examples of things to have on your site to invite people back are: online placement of accounts, online payment options, a free newsletter, 24 hour online reports, monitoring or status reports, and email communications with clients and debtors.

You will want to learn all you can about search engine placement, key words, meta tags and descriptions in order to submit your site to the search engines. Again, if you don't have the time or the inclination to do this, you can hire someone to do it for you. See the Resource section of this book for website designers, hosting and updating services you can choose from.

Building your website summary

Get a domain name

Arrange for monthly hosting

Create website

Upload website

Promote your website

CHAPTER TWENTY-SIX
EXCUSES FROM CLIENTS

This invoice has to be approved by another department.

We're waiting for our customer to pay us.

We did not receive the product or service.

There's something wrong with the product.

The check is waiting to be signed.

We did not receive an invoice, statement, etc.

The bookkeeper is sick or on vacation.

The computer is down.

You're not on my list.

Accounts Payable only takes calls on Tuesdays between 1 and 3.

FUNNIEST AND STRANGEST EXCUSES

These are real excuses told to me by debtors in my years of being a collector:

I lost my glasses and can't read my mail.

My car is broken down and the nearest mailbox is 10 miles away!

That person is deceased, then a week later, when you call the number, that person is not home right now or answers the phone.

I didn't know I had to pay that bill.

I was robbed of my mail at the post office while trying to mail your check.

When I got home I couldn't find my checkbook. As soon as I find my checkbook, I will mail your check.

WHAT YOU CAN SAY

"The check is in the mail"

What day did you mail it? How much was the check for? Can I have the check number please?

"I already paid"

Great! When did you pay? Did you mail the payment or make it in person? Who did you make the payment to? How did you pay, check, money order, credit card? Do you have a fax where you can fax me a copy of your receipt? Here is my fax number, please have your bank fax me a copy of the front and back of that check.

"I don't have any money"

Are you working? How are you paying this phone bill or your rent, food, etc.? Can you borrow $5.00 to make a good faith payment on this account until this hardship is over?

"I don't have a job"

How are you living? Who pays your bills?

"I am sick and have medical bills"

How are you paying your medical bills? Set up a payment plan.

"I'm divorced and my ex is supposed to pay that bill"

Great, just send me a copy of the divorce decree that states that and we will remove you from this account and pursue the appropriate person.

"You're harassing me!"

This is the first time, I've called you, how have I harassed you? I can take your payment right now over the phone and never have to call you again. What would make you feel like you are not being harassed?

"My wife (husband) handles that"

What is their name? May I speak to them please?

If they tell you they are at work, ask for the work number or if not, ask when they will be home. Also, if you call back another day and get a machine, you can leave a message for the spouse and state that the spouse said they handled this matter, so you need to speak to them.

"I'll Try"

Do you get paid on Thursday or Friday? So, you can send $50 on Saturday? If they say no, ask if they can send $25 and go down from there. Ask if they will mail it or if you should call back to take the payment over the phone. If they say they will mail the payment, call on Friday or Saturday to verify the payment was sent and ask for a check number.

"I'll pay in full when I get my tax refund"

Who did your taxes? When will they be done? How much are you getting back? Is the IRS sending you a check or doing a direct deposit to your bank account?

"When I have some extra money I will pay you"

Do you get paid on Friday? So you can send $25 on Saturday, I will send you an envelope for your payment. Also always send a confirmation of payment letter.

"I can't get a loan"

Can you ask a family member to loan you enough money to make a good faith payment? Can you check with your employer about an employee advance?

"Hold on a minute" then they disconnect you

Call back and leave a message. Send a letter with a payment envelope. Keep following up with collection calls.

"My insurance company should have paid that"

Who is your insurance company? Can you contact them and ask them to call me about this matter? NOTE: In the meantime contact your client to get information on why this was denied through insurance so you can call the debtor back with that information and set up a payment plan.

"I have more important bills to pay"

Depending on what this bill is for; credit card, auto loan, vet bill, depends on how to answer this one. You can also tell them their credit is very important, and this will affect them for some time and in their future if they don't set up some type of payment arrangement.

"We're filing for bankruptcy"

Please fax me the paperwork and give me your attorneys name and number so I may contact them.

"Invoice has to be approved by another department"

Which department? Who approves them? May I speak to that person? Try to get a direct number.

"We are waiting for our customers to pay us"

Your terms are net 30, and this bill is over 180 days old. Just because you do not have a good credit policy with your clients, that should not reflect on your credit. You may want to place your past due customer with a collection agency before you ruin the reputation of your company by not paying your vendors.

"There was a problem with the service or product"

It has been 180 days since you received it and our client or our office has never received any information that there was a dispute. What was the problem?

Resolve the problem by being a mediator with debtor, and client, also see if there is a contract, they may have only had a certain amount of time to dispute.

"There's something wrong with the product"

You had 30 days to return the product once you had received it, it has now been 180 days so you are required to pay for it. Send them a copy of the terms, agreement or contract showing this or showing whatever the case may be.

"We did not receive the product or service"

Request a proof of delivery from the shipper and or copy of agreement or contract for services from client.

"The check is waiting to be signed"

Where is the check? Who signs it? Is that person there? What is their name? May I speak to that person?

"We did not receive the invoice or statement"

What is your fax number? Fax information over right away and call right back.

"The bookkeeper is sick or on vacation"

Who is doing her job while she is out? May I speak to the owner? Get the owners name, if they won't give it to you, look them up online and get it. Call back and leave messages for that person.

"The computer is down"

When will it be up? I will call back in the morning. - And call back!

"You're not on my list"

What list is that? How do I get on the list? Who makes the list? May I speak to that person?

"Accounts payable only takes calls on Tuesdays between 1 and 3"

Call back Tuesdays from 1-3. But send a letter so they will have it before Tuesday and get a name of the Accounts Payable person.

CHAPTER TWENTY-SEVEN
STATE CONTACTS AND REQUIREMENTS

ALASKA

Contact P.J. Gingras
Dept. of Commerce, Community &
Exonomic Development
Division of Occupational Licensing
Box 110806
Juneau, AK 99811-0806
Phone 907-465-2695
Fax 907-465-2974
p.j._gingras@commerce.state.ak.us
www.commerce.state.ak.us/occ/
pcoa.htm

ARIZONA

Original license application is $1500
Branch office application is $500
Original license renewal is $600
Branch office renewal is $200
To change a managers name on a
license is $250
Robert Charleton
Division Manager
Financial Services
2910 N 44th Street, Suite 310
Phoenix, AZ 85018
Phone 602-255-4421 ext. 129
Fax 602-381-1225
License required.
Bond is required.
www.azdfi.gov
licensing@azdfi.gov

ARKANSAS

License $125
You pay an additional $15 per
collector
Jo Ann Quirk, Executive Director
State Board of Collection Agencies
523 S. Louisiana St. Suite 460
Little Rock AR 72201
Phone 501-376-9814
Fax 501-372-5383
License is required.
www.asbca.org
jwilson@asbca.com

CALIFORNIA

Secretary of State
1500 11th St.
Sacramento CA 95814
Phone 916-653-7244
No license is required

COLORADO

Original license is $300
License renewal is $190
You pay an additional $6 per collector
Laura E. Udis, Executive Director
Collection Agency Board
1525 Sherman St. 5th Floor
Denver CO 80203
Phone 303-866-5706
Fax 303-866-5691
License is required.
cab@state.co.us
www.ago.state.co.us/CAB.htm

CONNECTICUT

License and renewal is $400
William Naha Jr, Director
Consumer Credit Division
Department of Banking
260 Constitution Plaza
Hartford CT 06103
Phone 860-240-8200 Ext. 8201
Fax 860-240-8178
License is required.
Jean.wright@po.state.ct.us
www.state.ct.us/dob

DELAWARE

Registration fee is $75
Branch office fee is $25
Division of Revenue
820 N. French St.
Wilmington, DE 19801
Phone 302-577-8205
Fax 302-577-8202
Registration required.
www.state.de.us/revenue/index.htm

DISTRICT OF COLUMBIA

Vandy Jamison, Program Manager
Corporations Division
Department of Consumer and
Regulatory Affairs
941 North Capital Street NE
Washington, DC 20002
Phone 202-442-4400
Fax 202-442-9445
No license or registration is required.
dcra@dc.gov
http://dcra.dc.gov

FLORIDA

Registration and renewal is $200
Dan Saxton, Director
Division of Finance
Department of Banking and Finances
Office of Financial Institutions and

Securities Regulation
200 E. Gaines Street
Tallahassee, FL 32399-0375
Phone 850-410-9805
Fax 850-410-9431
Registration is required.
Electronic_licensing@dfs.state.fl.us
www.dbf.state.fl.us/licensing/licensing-h.html

GEORGIA

Secretary of State
214 State Capitol
Atlanta GA 30334
Phone 404-656-2881
Fax 404-656-0513
No license or registration required.
sosweb@sos.state.ga.us
www.sos.state.ga.us and
www.georgiacorporations.org

HAWAII

Application is $25
Registration is $40
Lee Ann Teshima
Professional and Vocational Licensing
Division
Department of Commerce and
Consumer Affairs
Box 3469
Honolulu HI 96801
Phone 808-586-2694
Fax 808-586-2689
Registration is required.
collection@dcca.hawaii.gov
www.hawaii.gov/dcca/areas/pvl/
programs/collection

IDAHO

Permit and renewal is $50
Application and renewal is $20
Collector license is $20
Collector registration (per collector)
$20
Michael Larsen, Bureau Chief
Department of Finance
700 West State Street
Second Floor
Boise ID 83720-0031
Phone 208-332-8000
Fax 208-332-8098
Collection Agency Licensing:
Phone 208-332-8002
Fax 208-332-8089 or 208-332-8099
finance@fin.state.id.us

ILLINOIS

Application fee for a certificate of
registration and renewal (which is
good for 3 years) is $750 each.
Branch office registration fee and
renewal (which is also good for 3
years) is $250
Professional Services Section
Department of Professional Regulation
320 W Washington St. 3rd Floor
Springfield IL 62786
Phone 217-785-0800
Fax 217-782-7645
Registration is required.
www.dpr.state.il.us/who/coll.asp

INDIANA

Original and renewal application is
$100
License fee is $30
Branch office fee is $30
Lorraine Bigsbee, Deputy Commis-
sioner of Collection Agencies
Securities Division
Office of the Secretary of State
302 W Washington St Rm E111
Indianapolis IN 46204
Phone 317-232-6681
Fax 317-233-3675
License is required.
www.in.gov/sos/securities/
apps_forms.html

IOWA

If collections exceed $25,000 you
must pay a $10 fee and notify the
Iowa Department of Economic
Development
200 East Grand Ave.
Des Moines, IA 50309
Phone 515-242-4700
Fax 515-242-4809
Registration required.
info@iowalifechanging.com
www.iowalifechanging.com

KANSAS

Office of State Bank Commissioner
700 SW Jackson Suite 300
Topeka, KS 66603
Phone 785-296-2266
No license or registration required.
www.osbckansas.org

KENTUCKY

Secretary of State
State Capitol Building
Room 150
Frankfort KY 40601
Phone 502-564-3490
Fax 502-564-5687
No license or registration is required.

LOUISIANA

Licensing and renewal fee is $200
Buckli Broussard, Executive Officer
Office of Financial Institutions
PO Box 94095
Baton Rouge LA 70804-9095
Phone 225-922-2592
Fax 225-925-4524
License is required to collect and
solicit.

MAINE

License and renewal is $400
Branch office license is $200
William N Lund, Director
Office of Consumer Credit Regula-
tion
35 State House Station
Augusta ME 04333
Phone 207-624-8527
Fax 207-582-7699
License is required.
www.state.me.us/pfr/ccp/
ccp_index.htm

MARYLAND

Each location must pay $400
Mary Louise Price, Chairperson
Department of Labor, Licensing and
Regulation
Commissioner of Financial Regula-
tion
500 North Calvert Street, Suite 402
Baltimore, MD 21202
Phone 410-230-6100
Fax 410-333-0475
License is required.
www.dllr.state.md.us/finance/

MASSACHUSETTS

License is $500
Dennis C. Otis, Chief Director of
Licensing
Massachusetts Division of Banks
One South Station
Boston, MA 02110
Phone 617-956-1500 ext. 551
Fax 617-956-1597
License is required.
Dennis.otis@state.ma.us
www.state.ma.us/dob/con_comp.htm

MICHIGAN

License fee $125
Linda Birch, Licensing Administrator
Collection Practices Board
Box 30018
Lansing MI 48909
Phone 517-241-9288
Fax 517-241-9280
License is required.
bcslic@michigan.gov
www.michigan.gov/cis/

MINNESOTA

License is $500
Renewal is $400
You must pay an additional $10 for
each collector
Jim Bernstein
Deputy Commissioner of Enforce-
ment and Licensing
Department of Commerce Licensing
Division
85 7th Place East
St. Paul, MN 55101-3165
Phone 651-296-6319 or 1-800-657-
3978
Fax 651-264-4107
License is required.
Licensing.commerce@state.mn.us
www.commerce.state.mn.us

MISSISSIPPI

Certificate of Authority is $500
Secretary of State
700 North Street
PO Box 136
Jackson, MS 39205
Phone 601-359-1350
Fax 601-359-1607
No license or registration is specifi-
cally required.
www.sos.state.ms.us

MISSOURI

Secretary of State
600 W. Main Street
Jefferson City, MO 65101
Phone 573-751-4936
Fax 573-526-4903
No license or registration required.
SOSMain@sos.mo.gov
www.sos.mo.gov/default.asp

MONTANA

Secretary of State
State Capital
Room 225
Helena MT 59620
Phone 406-444-2034
Fax 406-444-3976
No license of registration required.

NEBRASKA

Original license is $200
Renewal is $100
Branch offices are $50
Renewal for branch offices are $35
Scott Moore, Secretary of State
Cynthia Coleman, Admin.
Collection Agency Licensing Board
1305 State Capital Building
Phone 402-471-8606
Fax 402-471-2530
License is required.
Nikki.gordon@sos.ne.gov
www.sos.state.new.us/business/
collection

NEVADA

Applicatioin is $250
License is between $100-$300, call to
find out
Renewal fee is $200
Branch office applications are $125
Renewal for branch offices are $100
L. Scott Walshaw, Commissioner
Financial Institutions Division
Department of Commerce
406 E 2nd St.
Carson City NV 89710
Phone 775-684-1830
Fax 775-684-1845
License is required.
www.fid.state.nv.us

NEW HAMPSHIRE

Secretary of State
204 State House
Concord NH 03301
Phone 603-271-3242
Fax 603-271-6316
No license or registration is required.
www.state.nh.us/sos

NEW JERSEY

Filing fee and certificate to do
business is $25
James Fruschine
Chief of Filing Services
Division of Commercial recording
Department of State
NJ Division of revenue
Collection Agency Bond Section
PO Box 453
Trenton, NJ 08625
Phone 609-292-9292
Fax 609-530-8292
No license or registration required.
www.state.nj.us/treasury/revenue/
filecollagbond.htm

NEW MEXICO

Origina license is $500
Renewal is $300
Financial Institutions Division
2550 Cerrillos Road, 3rd Floor
Santa Fe, NM 87505
Phone 505-476-4885
Fax 505-476-4670
License is required.
RLDFID@state.nm.us
www.rld.state.nm.us.fid

NEW YORK – NEW YORK CITY ONLY

License and renewal are $75
Keith W. Stack, Deputy Secretary of
State for Business & Licensing
Services
Division of Licensing Services
84 Holland Avenue
Albany, NY 12208-3490
Phone 518-474-4429
Fax 518-473-6648
licensing@dos.state.ny.us
www.dos.state.ny.us

City of Buffalo

Ann Kilmurray
Division of Licensing
Room 113, City Hall
Buffalo, NY 14202
Phone 716-851-4951
Fax 716-851-4952

New York City

Jules Polonetsky, Commissioner
Department of Consumer Affairs
42 Broadway
New York NY 10004
Phone 212-487-4444
Fax 212-487-4090

NORTH CAROLINA

Application fee is $500
Frederick H. Mohn, Deputy Commissioner
Special Services Division
North Carolina Department of
Insurance
Agent Services Division
1204 Mail Service Center
Raleigh, NC 27699-1204
Phone 919-733-7487
Fax 919-715-3794
Permit is required.
www.ncdoi.com

NORTH DAKOTA

License is $200
Branch office is $50
Timothy J. Karsky, Commissioner
Department of Financial Institutions
2000 Schafer Street, Suite G
Bismarck, ND 58501-1204
Phone 701-328-9933
Fax 701-328-9955
dfi@state.nd.us
www.discovernd.com

OHIO

Secretary of State
Client Services Center
30 E. Broad Street, Lower level
Columbus, OH 43215
Phone 614-466-3910 or 1-877-767-6446
Fax 614-644-0649
No license or registration is required.
busserv@sos.state.oh.us
www.state.oh.us/sos

OKLAHOMA

Secretary of State
101 State Capitol
Oklahoma City OK 73105
Phone 405-521-3911
Fax 405-521-3771
No license required.

OREGON

Registration is $350
Renewal is $75
James Krueger, Program Manager
Collection Agency Program
Collection Licensing
Division of Finance and Corporate
Securities
PO box 14480
Salem, OR 97309-0405
Phone 503-378-4140
Fax 503-947-7862
Registration is required.
Dcbs.dfcsmail@state.or.us
http://dfcs.oregon.gov

PENNSYLVANIA

Secretary of the Commonwealth
Department of State
302 North Office Bldg.
Harrisburg PA 17120
Phone 717-787-7630
Fax 717-787-1734
No license or registration required.

RHODE ISLAND

Secretary of State
Room 218, State House
Providence, RI 02903
Phone 401-277-2357
Fax 401-277-1356
No license or registration required.
www.state.ri.us

SOUTH CAROLINA

Secretary of State
Wade Hampton Building
PO Box 11350
Columbia SC 29211
Phone 803-734-2170
Fax 803-734-2164

SOUTH DAKOTA

Secretary of State
State Capitol
Second Floor
500 East Capital Ave. Suite 204
Pierre SD 57501
Phone 605-773-3537
Fax 605-773-6580
No license required.
sdsos@state.sd.us
www.state.sd.us/sos

TENNESSEE

Application is $150
License is $600
Jean Blunkall, Adminstrative Director
Tennessee Collection Service Board
Davey Crockett Tower
500 James Robertson Pkwy, 6th Floor
Nashville, TN 37243
Phone 615-741-1741
Fax 615-741-1245
License is required.
Jean.w.blunkall@state.tn.us
www.state.tn.us/commerce/boards/
collect/

TEXAS

Nina Weston
Legal Support Unit
Secretary of State
Corporations Section
PO box 13697
Austin, TX 78711
Phone 512-463-555
Fax 512-463-5709
No license required.
sosdirect@sos.state.tx.us
www.sos.state.tx.us/corp

UTAH

Lorena Riffo-Jensen, Director
Department of Commerce
Division of Corporations and Commercial Code
160 E. 300 S.
Salt Lake City, UT 84111
Phone 801-530-4849
Fax 801-530-6438
License required. Bond required.
corpucc@utah.gov
www.commerce.utah.gov/cor/ca.html

VERMONT

Secretary of State, Corporations Division
81 River St. Drawer 09
Montpelier, VT 05609
Phone 802-828-2386
Fax 802-828-2853
No license is required.
bpoulin@sec.state.vt.us
www.sec.state.vt.us/corpsindex.htm

VIRGINIA

Secretary of the Commonwealth
830 East Main St. 14th floor
Richmond, VA 23219
Phone 804-786-2441
Fax 804-371-0017
No license required.
socmail@governor.virginia.gov

WASHINGTON

Original application is $650
Branch office is $350
Harumi Tolbert, Program Manager
Department of Licensing
Collection Agency Board
Department of Licensing
Collection Agency Board
PO Box 9034
Olympia, WA 98507-9034
Phone 360-664-1389
Fax 360-570-7875
License is required.
Collect@dol.wa.gov

WEST VIRGINIA

Registration is $15
Susan Tabor
Department of Tax and Revenue
PO Box 2666
Charleston WV 25330-7666
Phone 304-558-8500
Fax 304-558-1990
License is required.
www.state.wv.us/taxdiv

WISCONSIN

License is $200
Jean Plale
Supervisor of Licensed Financial
Services
Department of Financial Institutions
Licensed Financial Services Section
4th Floor
345 W Washington Ave.
Madison, WI 53703
Phone 608-261-7578
Fax 608-267-6889
License is required.
www.wdfi.org

WYOMING

License is $500
Branch office license is $500
Renewal on both is $300
WYOMING
Collection Agency Board
Sharon Smith, Administrative Assistant
Department of Audit, Div. Of Banking
Herschler Building 3 East
122 West 25th Street
Cheyenne WY 82002
Phone 307-777-3497
Fax 307-777-3555
License is required.
maitchison@wyaudit.state.wy.us
http://audit.state.wy.us/banking

U.S. Territories

Puerto Rico

Bureau of Enforcement
Department of Consumer Affairs
Commonwealth of Puerto Rico
Box 41059 Minillas Station
San Juan PR 00940
Phone 787-721-3280
Fax 787-726-5707

U.S. Virgin Islands

Andrew Rutnik, Commissioner
Department of Licensing & Consumer
Affairs
Golden Rock Shopping Center
Christiansted, St. Croix, VI 00820
Phone 340-774-3130
Fax 340-776-8303

CHAPTER TWENTY-EIGHT
TIPS FOR SUCCESS

Every new business has its challenges, if starting your own collection agency is your first venture as an entrepreneur there are some tips I would like to share with you that can help remove some frustration, and feelings of being overwhelmed for you in your new venture. Being a bill collector is hard enough, any help I could get when I started out was appreciated and I want to share those tips with you.

Handle each piece of paper or mail only once. Read it, take action on it and file or throw it away. The more times you shuffle a piece of paper back into your in box or "to do" pile, the more overwhelming the mundane things become. Don't put off tasks that you find challenging or that you don't like to do. Do those things first and you will have peace of mind and it will be done.

Capitalize on each persons uniqueness. When you have people working for you encourage education and growth. You can teach someone something and help them do something more efficiently but you cannot change them. Successful managers know that the challenge is not to change or perfect people to how you want them to be but to capitalize on each persons traits that make them unique.

Keep away from people who try to belittle your ambitions. Small people always do this but the really great make you feel that you, too, can become great. – *Mark Twain*

Don't wait. If you wait to be completely knowledgeable or perfect at something before believing you can do it, you will never do it. When you start your collection agency, stretch yourself, educate yourself, and see yourself as an agency owner.

Network. Be open to networking even if you have never done it before. Always have business cards with you, on vacation, at the store or at a business function. Become involved with different groups, and even online or email groups. They all provide opportunities for the exchange of information and letting someone else know about your business.

Find a mentor. Find someone you admire and see as a leader. Why are they successful, what do they do that you can learn from?

Do unto others as you would have them do to you. Treat others with respect. Always use sound business ethics in all your dealings and you will be successful.

Treat your staff and employees fairly. Your employees are going to be the "front line" of your business. Their opinion of you and your agency, including how you treat them will reflect on your business. Happy employees are enthusiastic and productive employees. Be respectful and give credit when credit is due.

Just do it. If you are reading this book your thinking about starting your own business. Do the research, take the time to really sit and think, make notes and you will see your business starting to take shape. Stay on course and keep thinking about it and asking questions and you will do it sooner than you think.

Top 25 Success Tips

1. Never burn your bridges.
2. Dress well.
3. Under promise and over deliver
4. SMILE
5. Know when to say NO
6. Don't gossip
7. Look people in the eye
8. LISTEN
9. Have a firm handshake
10. Ask questions
11. Be on time!
12. Stay calm
13. Be well prepared
14. Be honest and helpful
15. Offer praise
16. Be positive
17. Be forgiving
18. Be generous
19. Be persistent
20. Be loyal
21. Be a self-starter
22. Take responsibility
23. Be bold
24. Take care of yourself
25. Be proud

CHAPTER TWENTY-NINE
TELEPHONE COLLECTION TIPS

ADVANTAGES & TIPS FOR COLLECTING BY TELEPHONE

- Inexpensive – compared to personal visits and individually typed letters
- Immediate – Produces some sort of answer the moment the contact is made.
- Personal – Allows an exchange between two people.
- Informative – Allows you to ask questions, obtain information and take appropriate action.
- Flexible – Approach can be varied as changing situations demand
- It should result in agreement as to what is to be done
- Use voice mail or answering messages and speak slowly
- Always be courteous
- When asked why you are calling, never say it is in regards to a debt, regarding an invoice is better.
- Create a sense of urgency by leaving a deadline time to hear from them
- Get the name of a person in charge of issuing checks or paying bills
- Ask for the best time to call them in the future
- Leave complete messages, your name, company name, phone number, and the request for a return call
- Get the name of the person taking the message
- Ask when the person you need to speak with will be back and call at that time
- Ask for a cell or work number, you will be surprised how many times someone will give you the number if you just ask for it.

CHAPTER THIRTY

COLLECTION SERVICES AGREEMENT EXAMPLE #1

Collection Agency agrees to the following terms and conditions:

That all collection efforts will be carried out in compliance with all applicable federal, state and local laws.

All monies collected will be remitted to the client with their monthly statement.

The Client, agrees to the following terms and conditions:

The Client agrees to report all payments, bankruptcy notices, and any and all communications from the debtor or any third party.

Once an account has been placed for collection with the Agency, the Client will stop all collection efforts on the account.

The Client agrees to provide copies of invoices, checks or statements that will verify the debt, if requested by the debtor or the Agency as needed.

The Client agrees to pay any commission or court costs owed upon receipt of our monthly statement. Once accounts are placed, commission is due if COLLECTION AGENCY collects, finds bill was paid previously or resolves account and client decides to write off or close account.

This agreement shall remain in effect for one full year from the date of signing, and unless terminated in writing by either party with a ninety- (90) day notice it shall automatically be renewed from year to year.

Collection Agency

NAME/President _____

Signature _____ Date _____

Company Name _____

Type of business _____

Signature _____ Date _____

Title: _____

Facsimile signatures shall be sufficient unless originals are required by a third party.

COLLECTION SERVICES AGREEMENT EXAMPLE #2

COLLECTION AGREEMENT

This Collection Agreement, made this __ day of _____, _____, by and between M.A.D. Collection Agency, through the authorization of Michelle A. Dunn, President, hereinafter known as "Agency," and _____, hereinafter known as "Client," sets forth the following terms and conditions:

The Agency agrees to:

Carry out all collection efforts in compliance with all applicable federal, state, and local laws.

Remit all monies collected to the client along with their monthly statement.

Collection rate is 25% of what is collected. Accounts over one year old or under $75 are 50%. Second placements are 50%. Returned merchandise/equipment as payment of claim: 50% of normal fee.

The Client agrees to:

Report all payments, bankruptcy notices, and any communications from the debtor directly to the Agency upon the client's receipt or knowledge of their existence.

Immediately stop all collection efforts by the Client, and to provide copies of any paperwork that will verify the debt, as requested by the debtor or Agency.

Pay any and all commission owed upon receipt of the Agency's monthly statement.

Pay any and all commissions owed to the Agency if:

- the Agency directly collects any monies due to the Client by the debtor on this account,

- the Agency finds that the account was previously paid by the debtor,

- the client withdraws the account after demand for payment has been made, or

- the client receives any monies directly from the debtor.

Payment's made directly to you will be invoiced subject to the standard rates. MAD Collection Agency invoice payment terms are "Payable upon receipt"

This Collection Agreement represents a legal binding contract between the Agency and Client, and all of its terms and conditions are enforceable by law. This contract remains valid unless terminated by either party with a ninety- (90) day notice.

Seen and agreed to as follows:

Agency:

My Collection Agency

Michelle Dunn, President _____ Date _____

Client:

Name of Company: _____

Signature _____ Date _____

Title _____

COLLECTION PLACEMENT FORM

My COLLECTION AGENCY

PO Box 123

Plymouth, NH 03264

To place accounts electronically go to www.myagency.com

Phone (603) 744-0000 Fax (603) 794-0000

Name _____ Amount due $ _____

Contact name If this is a business_____

Address_____

_____

City/State/Zip _____

Phone(s) _____

Date of Service _____

Last Pay Date _____

Mail Returned: Yes   No

Social Security # _____ DOB _____

Your Company Name _____ Date _____

Address_____

_____

City/State/Zip _____

Contact Name_____ Phone _____

Email _____ Fax _____

SAMPLE "THANK YOU FOR YOUR INTEREST IN MY AGENCY" LETTER

December 6, 2006

Frank's Heating & Air Conditioning

123 Main Street

Chicago IL 60614

Dear Frank Brown:

Thank you for your interest in My Collection Agency!

When you place an account in our collection program we begin collection proceedings immediately. We charge a 25% commission on money that we Collect, if the debt is under $75.00 or over one year old we charge a 50% commission on what we collect. The enclosed "What to do when you receive a collection notice" pamphlet is sent to all customers with the initial collection letter.

We also handle collections on customers that are past due that you would continue to do business with but that need some basic collection action taken. Either as a collection account or in our A/R Outsourcing program.

To place an account with us, simply mail or fax the enclosed Collection Placement Form. You can also call in your information or e-mail it to michelle@madagency.com . To place accounts online go to www.myagency.com. You can also fax or mail copies of bad checks, statements, invoices etc. The basic information that we need is name, address, phone and amount owed. We also offer credit reporting, skip tracing, A/R Outsourcing and a Letter Service for an additional fee.

At My COLLECTION AGENCY we are certain we will more than meet your needs.

Sincerely,

My COLLECTION AGENCY

Michelle Dunn

President

SAMPLE FOLLOW UP LETTER

March 19, 2006

Bobs Animal Hospital

1 Main Street

Holderness NH 03245

Dear Bob:

Thank you for choosing My Collection Agency for your collection needs!

By the time you receive this letter your debtor has already been contacted.

Enclosed is my card, please call or email me anytime you have any

questions. I have also enclosed some other information on our services as

well as a Collection Agreement.

Please fill out and sign the collection agreement and mail or fax it back to us.

Our fax number is (603) 794-0000.

Sincerely,

My Collection Agency

Michelle Dunn

President

FOLLOW UP ON A LEAD LETTER

September 11, 2006

Blair Medical Center

1 Main Street

Holderness NH 03245

Dear Barbara:

I just wanted to follow up with you on the information I sent you about My Collection Agency.

Enclosed is my card, please let me know if you have any questions or need any further information.

I look forward to working with you and helping you lower your receivables!

Thank you!

My Collection Agency

Michelle Dunn

President

CHAPTER THIRTY-ONE

TIPS FOR YOUR CLIENTS ON HOW TO AVOID BAD DEBT

The biggest tip I can give you is (shameless plug here) to purchase my book, *Become the Squeaky Wheel, a Credit & Collections Guide for Everyone.* This book is for business owners or business startups so they can make more money by just having a credit policy in place. If you know what your clients can be doing differently to avoid bad debt, you should share that information with them. This will help them, help you and show them that you know what you are talking about. They will see a more smoothly running credit department in house and a higher success rate on bad debt from you, their collection agency. Resulting in a happy customer who will tell everyone he knows about you. You can even give this book as a "thank you for your business" gift to your clients.

Here are some tips to get you started:

GET MORE THAN THE P.O. BOX

To increase an agency's chances of tracking down an individual or business, always ask for the customer's physical address, phone number and social security number. Also, ask for employment information including a phone number. All of this information will be helpful when tracking down individuals even if they have closed their P.O. Box or changed their address and phone number.

GET A SIGNED CREDIT APPLICATION AND CHECK CREDIT

Fend off collection problems from the start by running a credit check on new clients and by discussing your prices, service fees and payment requirements with new customers before your do any work. Carefully check credit references of each new account and don't extend more credit that the firm can handle.

EXPLAIN TRANSACTION TERMS THOROUGHLY

When extending credit, make sure that customers know when you expect payment, and clearly detail any credits or penalties for early or late payments.

FOLLOW UP ON OVERDUE ACCOUNTS

Make sure to promptly send statements and reminders of payment due dates. Making phone calls is necessary.

INSTITUTE A SERIES OF OVERDUE NOTICES

You should schedule regular written and oral reminders before even considering a collection agency. Check out "The First Book of Effective Collection Agency Letters & Forms" or even "How to help you Get Paid, Credit & Collection Forms & Letters", you can use the letters in these books or use parts of them to create your own series.

SET AN ABSOLUTE DATE AND STICK TO IT

As a final step, set an absolute date before the account is turned over to a collection agency. Do not extend this date, but do give the debtor warning of this final payment date. Maybe send a certified letter.

WHAT NOT TO DO

Don't tell your friends at the monthly Chamber meeting that the customer is a deadbeat, and don't plaster online bulletin boards or mailing lists with notes telling the world that your customer is a bad credit risk.

Don't hang copies of bad checks around town or in your place of business. If you do things like these, you can get yourself sued. You can also get yourself into legal hot water by making threats, using harassing or abusive language, making collection calls at odd hours or too often, or by making false statements about what will happen if the debtor doesn't pay. Creditors need to be aware of and educated about the FDCPA.

FREQUENTLY ASKED QUESTIONS

Q. *Does the age of the debt make it more difficult to collect?*

A. Yes, the older the debt is, the harder it is to collect. That is why some agencies charge more for older debts.

Q. *Is there a special software I can buy to install in my computer to skip trace?*

A. Not that I am aware of, if you hear of any please let me know! There are a lot of online skip tracing sites you can use such as:
www.flatrateinfo.com
www.accurint.com
You can find more at www.credit-and-collections.com

Q. *What do you think about charging service charge/skip tracing charge to clients after commission?*

A. I think that is up to the agency.

Q. *What Insurance coverage would I need?*

A. That would depend on what state you're in and what is required. It will also depend on how large your agency is. If you are a member of The American Collectors Association, you can purchase insurance through a company they deal with that deals with collection agencies. I purchased mine through them for a while but then purchased it through my local insurance company. Be sure they are familiar with the laws in relation to collection agencies.

Q. *How do you report to the major credit bureaus?*

A. You would need to become a member of a credit bureau such as
- www.equifax.com
- www.experian.com
- www.transunion.com

Q. *What do you mean by debt buying?*

A. Some agencies purchase debt rather than get accounts from clients to work on a commission basis. You can check out purchasing debt at wwww.chargeoffclearinghouse.com. Louise Epstein has over twenty years of experience in the debt business, including executive-level structuring, issuing, managing and selling and she is very helpful and friendly.

Q. *Does NSF Check Collection just mean collection of bad checks?*

A. Yes but NSF could also mean checks from a closed account.

Q. *What types of services do you include in the promotional packet?*

A. We list all of our services in the packets we send out so potential clients know what we offer and the cost of them.

Q. *Do I need to belong to American, CA Collection Association or National Trade Association?*

A. You don't "need" to but I would recommend it. It lets your clients know you have integrity and have to follow the laws of the FDCPA. Being a member of The American Collectors Association gives you the following benefits:

- Tailored, accurate risk management products: insurance, bonding, and licensing services
- On-target assistance in complying with industry laws and regulations
- Reduced rates for educational seminars, teleseminars, training programs and publications
- Access to timely information critical to success in the collection industry

And also:
- Legislative and Compliance Support
- Education & Information
- Business Services
- Special Programs

More from "Ask Michelle" If you have a question you want to "Ask Michelle" send her an email at michelle@michelledunn.com with Ask Michelle in the subject line. Please be aware all questions may be published in the free monthly newsletter, *Become The Squeaky Wheel*.

Q. *I have looked through your site and seen some of your books and other books that are good for collections. Seriously, is it hard to get started doing collections?*

A. The hardest part is knowing and following all the state and federal laws, and having your employees follow and know them as well. It is also hard dealing with unhappy people all day, when you make calls.

The basic business set up is the same as for any business, you need some specifics but you still need organization, follow up, and more. I started my agency when I had been a Credit Manager at a few different companies but I had never worked at a collection agency. I had dealt with them and placed accounts but that was all. I really loved it; you can see your accomplishments by how much money is collected. It is always a challenge.

Q. *I had a question concerning credit bureau reporting. I report to TransUnion and Equifax. I haven't found anyone that has been able to give me a definite answer (my TransUnion rep, my software vendor, etc). My software set-up requires that I put a number of months to report the debt which I currently have set to 84 months. We report the debt and then it continues to report each month if unpaid or paid after reporting for 84 months. It is my understanding that the debt will stay on the credit bureau record for 7 years from the date of delinquency. My question is should I change the number of months to report to a lesser number? Is there a standard?*

Example:

If I report a date of delinquency of 12/05/04, and it remains unpaid or is paid after the fact that should stay on the record until 12/05/11. If the account is placed with me in 12/05/05 and report in 02/05/05, according to my system set up of 84 months, I would be reporting it until 02/05/12 which would be incorrect.

Do you have any experience with this?

A. In my years of credit reporting, I always had to put the date the debt was incurred in addition to the date I received the account. I used Experian and before that TRW. Both asked me for both of these dates with each person I reported.

Q. *I just bought your book from Amazon and had a few questions. The first is do you have any sample letters to mail to potential customers in order to receive their business? Since I am starting very small and not experienced is it better to charge a flat rate if I collect their debts or do you charge for extra services. Are there any computer programs that supply letters, courses, easy software etc. (collection agencies for dummies)? Secondly how long do you generally take before you report the debts to the person's credit report? Lastly how do you report a person/company to a credit report agency such as Equifax? I spoke with them and they informed me I had to have at least 500 unpaid debts in order to work with them. Do you know of any other companies that do not require an amount?*

A. Thank you for buying my book! I do have some sample letters at http://www.credit-and-collections.com/startup-forms-docs.html and they are free, one is a Sales letter to send to get their business, and the one under it, is a Thank you for becoming a client letter and is to send once you get their business.

You can charge a flat rate, some agencies charge a monthly fee based on number of accounts, dollar amount, age and other factors. I always charged a commission of 25% on what I collected. I charged a flat fee for different types of skip tracing and credit reporting.

I don't know of any software with letters but I have a book specific for Collection Agencies which is full of letters. You can check that one out here: http://www.michelledunn.com/book_firstbook.html it is the only book that I know of like it in the field at the moment. I also have "How to help you Get paid", which is collection forms and letters. That one is here: http://www.michelledunn.com/book_getpaid.html and I have another "Fast, Easy, Effective Letters, How to get your Customers to Pay" that is being edited and will be available soon. There are also some free letters with those forms I told you about and I will be uploading more soon. I don't know of a book Collection Agencies for Dummies, but they do mention me and my agency in Home Based Business for Dummies, but it is a very small part.

I have a special going right now for members of Credit & Collections, where they can get 30 minutes of email or phone consulting on

How to Start a Collection Agency for $50. There is a paid professional membership or a free membership option and then you can ask as many questions and speak on the phone or use email for your consulting.

I used to wait about 60-90 days depending on the situation to report to the credit bureau. I didn't do anything in the first 30 days, and then I sent letters for 30 more days letting them know this could and would affect their credit if they didn't pay. I tried to give people extra time if I thought they would really pay or they tried.

Try calling Experian, that is who I used, I had over 500 debts so I don't know if they had a limit or not.

Q. *Hello, Michelle I e-mailed you about a week ago asking you for some ideas about getting clients. I have reviewed some of the letters you have on credit and collections website and I was just wondering how long did it take for you to get your first collection account? Also what type of accounts will give me the best chance to succeed in this industry?*

A. I got my first client by calling local businesses and following up with them and asking them to try me even though they used someone else. I was so confident I would do a better job that they would stay, and they did and they referred others to me. The best way to get new clients is word of mouth.

I would even ask existing clients, once I had them to refer me to other businesses, and then I would contact them and say, So and so gave me your name because I do their collections and they thought you might be interested as well.

Q. *I've a question. I'm looking for some sort of generic contract. I've started an in-house collection agency that collects delinquent rents for properties. This will be a split contract between the properties and myself. Would you be able to direct me in the direction that I need to head. I've checked legal forms and have found absolutely nothing that pertains to us.*

A. I have some in my books and also have a free one at http://www.credit-and-collections.com/startup-forms-docs.html that you can use.

Q. *What kind of background do you need to start a collection agency - do you have to have worked in collections? Can I ask what you might expect to make as an annual income working a collection agency from home?*

A. If you have worked in collections, it helps because then you have some experience. I had never worked at a collection agency and I started one. I had done collections work though.

I believe, because I did this myself, you can teach yourself. I bought many books and read them and networked with collectors. That is where www.credit-and-collections came from. I started that group and website when I couldn't find a lot of information about starting my own agency.

If you're interested, you can join and just read the posts to learn from others, it's free either way. I did write my book about Starting a Collection Agency because so many people have asked me these same questions. When I first started out, I didn't make much money and kept my day job for about a year. But it is that way with any business you start. How much you make doing collection work is up to you, I know this is true because the more phone calls I made for example, rather than sending more letters, made me more money. Once I had clients, and did a good job, I stopped advertising because I was generating clients by of word of mouth advertising. It can absolutely be done.

Q. *I've recently started a collection agency. I have purchased two of your books so far and plan to buy some more. They have a lot of great information... I have a question on the envelopes should I only put my address and no name or is there something else I could put?*

A. If your agency name indicates that you are a debt collector, you cannot legally put the company name on the envelope. What I did was just put my mailing address. On some envelopes, I put M.A.D. and the mailing address, my agency was M.A.D. Collection Agency. So I could not put the collection agency part.

Q. *My company is looking to hire a corporate A/R, Collections person. Do you know of any industry website that might have job listings or a resume database? Thank you in advance for any advice you may be able to provide.*

A. Here are some resources for you, I hope they help! Good luck! Executive Recruiters in the Customer Contact Industry, which includes collections operations. You can find a few collections jobs on our website at www.teledevelopment.com/hotjobs.html, and we can certainly aid anyone looking for Management personnel in this arena.

In addition, you might try the following:

◆ www.nacm.com
◆ www.collectionindustry.com
◆ www.creditjobstoday.com

CHAPTER THIRTY-TWO
HANDLING COMPLAINTS

With the internet readily available to anyone there is a wealth of unlimited information available to consumers and debtors. This can often mean they are misinformed and this hurts consumer perceptions and understandings regarding debt collection. This has led to a recent increase in complaints against collection agencies in the 40% to 50% range, according to the Federal Trade Commission. The FTC has had an increase in complaints often times as a result of incorrect information debtors have found on websites. This means more time spent on responding to complaints by collection agencies. This is one of the main reasons it is imperative to educate consumers in regards to debt collection, their debts and the laws and regulations.

Some of the top complaints in 2006 filed with the Federal Trade commission:
- Calling the wrong person
- Calling a debtor at work when the debtor asked them not to
- Calling too early or too late
- Abusive practices

According to the FTC they received the highest number of complaints in the month of December 2006 with 69 out of 490 complaints being about collectors contacting the wrong person.

Some things you can do to help defer consumer complaints are:
- Verify you are contacting the correct person
- Verify the total amount that is owed
- Monitor collectors to avoid abusive practices
- Do not call at work once asked not to
- Do not contact debtors more than once a day
- Never reveal personal information to others
- Respond to a "cease & desist" letter
- Help educate consumers about debt collection practices

CHAPTER THIRTY-THREE
STARTING YOUR AGENCY FROM HOME

If you decide to start your collection agency from a home office, there are some things you should know. If you have never worked from home before, it is very different from working at an office. When you work from home you are alone most of the time, you need to motivate yourself to get the job done. This is where networking comes in, try to network or meet associates for coffee. I used to visit my clients or potential clients to "get out of the house". I would just make it a point to visit them and see how things were going, if they were happy with my services and if there was anything I could do for them. Sometimes I would bring them pens or post it notes with my company name on them. I would do the same with businesses that I wanted to become customers, I would visit them and bring pens, and my promotional red folders and get the name and business card of the person who handled the accounts receivable, then I would have a specific person to follow up with.

Another issue with working from home is motivation to work and not watch TV, or become distracted with TV or launry. I never had this problem, and you probably won't either. You know that building your business takes a lot of hard work and that you will be so busy, that watching TV won't cross your mind. Becoming successful and making enough money to live on was motivation enough for me. Try setting specific work hours and stick to them.

Try using to do lists for each week or even just each day. That helps you to motivate because you will have to get those things done.

One of the biggest challenges is family and friends, explain to your family and friends that you are WORKING. People think if you are home, you are home and not working, they will drop by to visit, invite you to do things when they aren't at work, because they think you are not at work either. I sat down with my kids and explained to them that I would be working from home, and what times. This did not stop them from hovering in my doorway when I was on the phone, but at least they were quiet. I would always get my children settled with homework, snacks, a movie or whatever they were going to be doing, and then announce, I am going back to work now for an hour, is everyone all set? Does anyone need anything? This worked out well for me. If the kids become rowdy, because no matter how much you prepare them, this still happens! I would stop working and go out there and ask what the problem was and spend a little time with them. I found if you spend some time with them, they get settled back down pretty quickly and you can get back to work. The are normally acting up because they want your attention, so if you give them some attention rather than yelling at them to be quiet because you are working, that works much better. I know this from experience. I used to yell from my office chair, "What is going on out there?" and "Stop fighting, if I have to come out there!" You know the routine.

I had a business line and a home line, so I set my hours from 8-5. I of course worked much more than that, but those were my "advertised" hours. I would not answer my business phone before 8 or after 5. That is why I had voice mail. I did not answer my house phone between 8-5 because I was working. If your family or friends start calling your business line because you are not answering your house phone, explain to them that this is because you are working. It seems silly, but I am sure you will end up having to do this. I had to do it so many times, and was really surprised with peoples perception of "working from home". No, I didn't catch Oprah today!

When you work from home and do a lot of your business tasks yourself, you will have to be extremely organized. I always would organize my desk, file my paperwork and organize my office on the weekends so that on Monday I could start with a relaxed stress free attitude. Until I started making collection calls of course! Anything to lower stress, such as being organized, is a blessing to a bill collector.

CHAPTER THIRTY-FOUR
SUCCESSFUL COLLECTION AGENCY REFERENCES

Successful Collection Agencies that used *How to Make Money Collecting Money, Starting a Collection Agency* as a Start-Up Guide!

Your Collection Solution, LLC
PO Box 164, Newtown PA 18940
866-497-1006 (Toll Free)
215-497-1006 (PA)
215-497-1050 (Fax)
www.yourcollectionsolution.com

"Michelle Dunn has helped to bring the collection industry to a more reputable light. Collection Agencies have taken a bad wrap in the past and she has helped to dignify our industry with her integrity and knowledge. Her books are well thought out, her website is helpful and her e-mail group serves as a wealth of knowledge to our industry."

-Jan Conte, Pres.

Your Collection Solution, LLC
Alpine-BAK Collections, Inc.
934 N University Dr, #117
Coral Springs, FL 33071
877-722-6670
Beth Keefe - President

"Michelle Dunn is a tremendous resource, her books, web site, and forums continue to lead us through our new business in collections. We are very thankful for all her help."

-Ken Keefe

1st American Credit Solutions, LLC
12954 Stonecreek Drive Suite F
Pickerington, Ohio 43147
888-322-1227

"I found Michelle Dunn's book to be very resourceful when starting my agency. It was informative and provided a lot of direction to all of the details that need to be attended to when starting an agency. My agency is 1 year old and we have over 150 clients. Thanks Michelle!"

-Valerie Freda, 1st American Credit Solutions, LLC

You have been an inspiration to me and my fiancée for our collection agency. We only collect on bad checks, but you have been of great help with your books and your website and all of the info you offer to our lists!

Theresa Jordan
Express Check Recovery Services
P.O.Box 364
Channelview, Texas 77530
Thomas J. Bim, President

The Abeja Group, LLC
4601 E. Fort Lowell, Suite 200
Tucson, AZ 85718
1-520-829-4438 Ext. 101
1-520-881-8707 Fax

Strategic Commercial Collections
Jacqueline Roskos
100 West Ridge Ave. Ste. I
Sharpsville PA 16150
(800)267-8889

I have been in the collection agency business for fifteen years, and have been a successful entrepreneur within 2 companies.

We enjoy what we do, and give all our attention to the accounts placed within our agency. All the hard work and professional skills have come a long way...

Singer, Bach & Associates Commercial Debt Recovery
Joseph Bryant
1200 N. El Dorado Place Suite E550
Tucson, AZ 85715
888-530-1010

Credit & Collections member, Norma Burns, tells how she started Burns & Carlisle:

Burns & Carlisle is a new collection agency, established in Feb 2005. Norma Burns is the owner of the company. She is located in Yantis Texas, home of the best Large Mouth Bass fishing lake in the United States, Lake Fork. Her agency specializes in medical and utility debt collections, and has clients in both Oklahoma and Texas.

Norma started her business on Feb 23, 2005. "It took me 2 months to get everything in place, software, advertising, phone lines, applications for credit bureau, electronic payments and more", says Burns. Norma then turned her focus to clients. She tried what most people recommended, "Cold Calling". It did not take long before she realized that this method of selling was a waste of time. "I rarely walked into a business and met with the individual that I needed to meet with. Instead, I got a lot of "she's out today, we do our collections in-house, she's busy and can not meet with you, can you mail us something, and so on" states Burns. She thought maybe the phone would yield better results. Her and her employee developed a strategy and designated territories. In no time at all her calendar was full of scheduled appointments. She then decided to hire sales reps to make the phone contacts – as it was time consuming and she had business rolling in that needed to be worked. Under the terms of her sales rep contract she is guaranteed to have a minimum of 12 appointments per month. That's over 100 clients per year if she gets them all, well worth the sales reps fee. Her reps are getting her approximately 6 appointments per week right now. She is signing clients right and left and that is because the sales rep sells the business and gets the interest, the brochure sells my business services, then Burns simply closes the deal with a signed contract. Her biggest fear is that she will grow too fast too soon – IMAGINE that being the concern of a new business! She now has 4 employees and her goal is 100 + clients by the end of this year.

In addition to this, Burns offers her staff 1% of all commission they bring into the company – under the same general terms of her sales rep contract. This is far better than a "finder's fee" because it does not take long before a collector sees the $ potential. She also increases her fee by 1% with her client to cover the collector's fee so she gains everything and loses nothing.

Burns finds it more effective to get clients over the phone than in person. She feels it is a real time saver when you know you will be meeting the person that makes the decisions and not the front office clerk. At Burns & Carlisle the rep will make the phone contact, send a brochure of her services, then follow-up and secure the appointment. Sometimes, they don't even want a brochure – they just make the appointment. If you've gotten that far, there is a good chance you've got the client. They are obviously shopping for an agency or they would not even take the time to meet with you. So you know when you get there they are interested to begin with. This method is very effective for me.

Norma Burns
Burns & Carlisle
P.O. Box 620, Yantis, Texas 75497
Phone: (800) 736-2182, Fax: (800) 951-7439
www.BurnsandCarlisle.com

Reprinted with permission from Norma Burns of Burns & Carlisle

When I grow up I want to be a Bill Collector

by David Ward, President, International Association of Commercial Collectors

(Reprinted with permission from the largest association of commercial collection professionals in the world.)

Nobody, with the possible exception of the second and third generation owners of agencies, ever graduated from their particular Institute of Learning or, for that matter, entered one saying "I am going to be a bill collector!" Let's face it; we don't get the respect that we deserve. How many of us have been at social gatherings and have been asked "What do you do for a living?" In the early days of my career in debt collection, I used to try to evade that question by saying something vague like "I work in credit", and hope that whomever I was speaking with would simply accept it and go away. Now, in my third decade in this business, I say "I own a collection agency". The reactions that statement solicits are amazing. The most common is "Gee, I hope you don't have my name". My usual reply to that is "I don't know, but I'll check Monday morning."

There are people that are actually willing to continue the conversation after finding out my occupation. I then go into the specifics, explaining that mine is a commercial collection agency. Of course I then have to explain the difference between consumer and commercial agencies. With no offense meant to our consumer agencies, the average person is less likely to know how a commercial agency operates. Some of them probably know first hand how consumer agencies operate, the others just know what they hear from disgruntled debtors, but the guy hiding under the couch is probably the subject of your skip trace department.

What these people do not realize is that the collection industry serves an important role in the U.S. economy by recovering billions in revenue for U.S. companies. Our industry saves the average American citizen somewhere between $300 and $400 each, per year. The average citizen saves hundreds of dollars but recoils when meeting a debt collector. What's wrong with that picture? We have a gigantic public relations problem. The general public sees bill collectors as the enemy. That couldn't be further from the truth. Now I'm not saying that we're all warm and fuzzy, but we certainly aren't the bad guys. The problem is that the wise-ranging perception is that we are trying to repossess children's lunchboxes, with the PB&J still inside! I know I'm preaching to the choir, but all we are doing is enforcing the promise that these people (our debtors) made when they obtained the goods and services for which they now have not paid.

Credit is simply based upon a promise to pay. When we get involved, someone broke a promise. That broken promise, if not enforced, will lead to a write off (see "billions" previous paragraph) by the credit grantor. The credit grantor, a business itself, will somehow have to make up that loss. The way the loss is usually made up is that it is passed on to the good paying customers in the form of a price increase. We all know that a price increase will keep rolling downhill until it lands in the consumer's pocket. The same holds true with consumer debt. It's something of a vicious cycle. We are the line of defense. We are holding those potential write offs to a minimum. We are keeping the cost of living down. Ok, maybe that is stretching it a bit but I'm sure we are responsible for holding down a percentage.

It is up to you, the Collection Professional, to begin to change that broad perception. You and I cannot do it overnight. The journey is long and challenging, yet even the longest journey beings with a first step. In order to travel we must embark. We must commit to movement, to action and to change.

CHAPTER THIRTY-FIVE
MOST FREQUENTLY ASKED QUESTIONS ABOUT STARTING A COLLECTION AGENCY

Q: Just bought your book on how to start a collection agency. I am basing this out of my home and I have to tell you I am a little nervous. I have been in the collection/credit industry for over 15 years. I have wanted my own business for about 10 years now. But I have always been afraid to do it. Your book inspired me. There is just so much to do to get started. I am afraid I am going to forget something. I am going to incorporate into an S corporation instead of sole proprietorship. I want to protect my assets just in case it doesn't work out. Is there anything you can tell me personally from your experience to give me more confidence. I have always been a driven, confident person but I think this is a little intimidating. I would like to get this up and running before the end of the year. Is there any good time to start or doesn't it matter? Well thanks for listening to me and I hope someday to be successful. Any help you can offer would be greatly appreciated.

A: Are you afraid that your business won't get off the ground or that you can't do the work? Do you have a business plan? There is one in my book and you can use it exactly how it is, if you like. You have a much higher chance of succeeding with a business plan than without one. Do you have a marketing plan? I put my marketing plan in the book as well, because when I started my agency I couldn't' find any plans for agencies and had to write my own. It took me a lot of time and research and that is why I included them in the book, so it could save anyone who purchased the book all of that time and research.

Q: Hi, I am currently a senior at a University. I am very interested in opening up a part-time agency from home when I graduate. I use to work for a agency over the summer and I know this business can be very rewarding. My question is how profitable do you think I can be by just starting out part-time from home? My ultimate goal is to be the #1 agency in the country, can you please offer me some advice. Thanks.

A: I opened my agency part time from my home when I started it, so I know you can do it. Your profit will depend on how much you streamline your work, and on the types of collections you do, for example you might only do commercial collections, which can make you more money than consumer, or you may want to just purchase debt. It is up to you and what you want to do.

Q: I was directed to your site as a result of looking for ways and steps to start my own collection agency. I currently live in a city where there is ample opportunity to start something like this. I do have a Business degree and a Sales Professional degree and would like to start my own personal business in collections. I would appreciate any information that you may be able to provide me with. I am mainly interested in how to obtain clients to collect for, and by looking at your website I discovered that you may be able to help me obtain this information.

A: I have quite a few free resources at http://www.credit-and-collections.com/startup-tips.html

You can also join my networking group at http://www.credit-and-collections.com/index.html to network and learn from others who are just starting their agencies as well as experts and other agency owners. Some of the members include collection software people, merchant account companies and other resources collection agencies use. I also offer Starting a Collection Agency consulting if you are interested. Also check out www.startingacollectionagency.com which is run by my good friend David Ward, he has a lot of really great information up on his site.

Q: I have been working in a collection agency for the past two years. I have collected on many credit card accounts. I have probably collected an estimated amount of dollars for this company that are close to $450K. All I am making is some hourly rate and some bonuses.
So now I am at the point where I want to do this for myself. I was researching my options and came across your organisation so here I am trying to get all the help and information I need to succeed at

becoming my own boss. The kind of help I need is how to get the clients- what is the best way to approach them?

A: You might want to start by checking out some information regarding starting your own agency, and depending on what state you are in, you may have to obtain a license. I have some free information at http://www.credit-and-collections.com/startup-tips.html and also my book "Starting a Collection Agency, How to make money collecting money" has a chapter about marketing, how to get clients and a full marketing plan you can use for yourself.

Q: My husband and I are in the process of starting our own Debt Collection Agency. I personally have over 20 years of experience in different phases of collections; however, my experience was in the area of working for someone else. We have read a book of yours and it was helpful. Now we would like to order The Premium Collections Kit (in Print form) for $119.95 as is notated on the computer plus any S&H (if any). Do the samples of form letters you show in your books apply to all States (we live in Florida) or is it just for New Hampshire? In other words, are the letters generic so-to-speak and legally appropriate? I am interested in the Credit & Collections Organization that you own. Are there local Chapters? Meetings?

A: Congratulations on starting your own agency! You can order the Premium Collections Kit at http://www.michelledunn.com/store/store.html and choose the print form and your shipping will be added to your order. All orders are processed and shipped within 24 hours and include delivery confirmation.

The letters are for all states, you would need to have your own letterhead to copy the letters onto, and in some states where they ask for your license number or physical address to be included on the letters, you would need to include that as well, but I am sure that would be part of your letterhead.

My Credit & Collections Association has a free membership and a paid Professional Membership, you can check out the website at www.credit-and-collections.com and sign up, there are also a lot of free resources at http://www.credit-and-collections.com/startup-tips.html

THE FIRST BOOK OF EFFECTIVE COLLECTION AGENCY LETTERS & FORMS

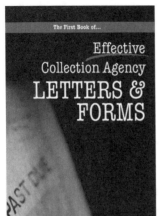

ISBN# 0-97066454-0

From the Author

Where can I find letters and forms to use for my Collection Agency? Right here!

Finally, a book of letters and forms specific to Collection Agencies! When you buy *The First Book of Effective Collection Agency LETTERS & FORMS*, you will have the tools you need to create and use debt collection letters effectively for your agency. Included in this book are collection agency letters and forms that you can use as is or modify to suit your needs, information on letter compliance for collection agencies, samples of forms, information on FDCPA and more.

This book was created as a companion to *How to Make Money Collecting Money, Starting a Collection Agency.*

I have had so many people ask me where they can find such letters and forms that I had to provide you with this information. There are many books written with letters, forms and contracts but they are for creditors and do not focus on Collection Agencies. I created this book so you could have some examples of letters agencies successfully use. This books is a guide for you to create or modify your debt collection letters to be more effective and help you collect more money. This book was not written or designed to provide legal advice, but as a guide to help you collect more money using letters and forms.

Some exciting information included in this book:
- How to use Debt Collection Letters Effectively
- Letter Compliance for Collection Agencies
- Collection Agency Letters
- Investigation Letters
- Easy Credit Forms
- FDCPA
- Mini-Miranda

and more!

Order your copy today of this great e-book and start collecting more money today!

HOW TO GET YOUR CUSTOMERS TO PAY

with Michelle Dunn

How to Get Your Customers to Pay E-Course

The Fast way to explode your Accounts Payable to increase your bottom line TODAY! Don't forget, professional Credit and Collections members receive a discount on this e-course, as well as other great benefits.

Course Outline

5 day collection e-course - Get an email each day for 5 days. Each lesson will walk you through a step-by-step process to get control of your accounts receivables.

Get Your Customers to Pay e-book - Free 126 page book of easy, effective letters to walk you through the "dunning" process.

Success Sheets – Includes a "Debt Collection Cheat sheet", an Excuses Sheet and Tips & Tricks Sheets with the "nuts & bolts" of exactly what you need to do to get paid legally. Ready to print and hang near your phone to assist you with collection calls starting today.

Monthly subscription to *Become the Squeaky Wheel Newsletter* - full of articles, tips, and resources that will help you in every aspect of your collection work.

Benefit of this course: The Fast way to explode your Accounts Payable to increase your bottom line TODAY!

Does your business have a collection policy for outstanding debts? Take the *How to Get Your Customers to Pay* e-course and find out how to use a credit policy to strengthen and protect your business!

Michelle Dunn, credit and collections expert, offers you:

Day 1 – Credit and collections policy information

Day 2 – Avoiding the Trash Can! Collecting with letters and getting your envelopes opened!

Day 3 – Effective collection phone calls

Day 4 – Excuses! Dealing with and responding to debtor excuses!

Day 5 – Your most important collection tool: Follow Up!

Each day you will also receive:

Easy Collection Tips & Resources.

Do not wait to start learning from this important course. Take the course so many others have taken with positive results.

"Many business owners dread making a debt collection call," explains Dunn. "This course will provide participants the opportunity to see and practice what is involved with these calls to prepare them for making calls to their own customers – an essential task for entrepreneurs who want their business to succeed in the long-term."

My name is Michelle Dunn and I am the founder of my Credit & Collections Association with thousands of members as well as the author of 5 books in my *Collecting Money Series*. I am the author of the *Ultimate Credit & Collections Handbook* published by Entrepreneur Press. I was a bill collector for 17 years and started and ran my own collection agency for 8 years. I was named as one of the Top 5 Women in Collections in 2007.

I wrote this Debt Collectors Collection Training System because I wanted to share with you some steps you can take to help make your business more profitable.

"Become the Squeaky Wheel" is a term that has been used by bill collectors for a very long time, that means – be a pest and get paid. In the Debt Collectors Collection Training System I will tell you how you can use a credit policy to collect the money that is owed to you now and prevent more bad debts in the future. If you are like me, you like to get paid for the work you do without having to also "work to get paid". My System will help you learn how you can "Become the Squeaky Wheel."

BECOME THE SQUEAKY WHEEL, A CREDIT & COLLECTIONS GUIDE FOR EVERYONE

From the author ...

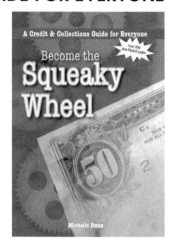

Over 100,000 businesses have slow or non-paying customers. How can you collect that money quickly and without to much effort? How can you keep the money coming in?

One of the things I like about collection work is that you can see your results. I also like making people happy and one of the things that makes people happy is receiving money. So I make my collection calls and send my letters and money comes in and everyone is happy, except maybe the person who had to send the money

I have been a Credit Manager at quite a few different companies and written credit and collection policies for many companies. I have tried to give you an example of some of those policies in this book. Some of the information may not work with your specific line of business but there is something for everyone in this book.

This can be used as a guide for your own credit policy. You can use parts of this policy or adjust any parts of it to fit your business. You can also just use parts of it or all of it.

I have included a procedure on what to do when you get a new customer, how to extend credit to them, how to read a credit report if you pull reports on new customers. What to do once you have credit approved customers and they don't pay, putting them on hold and procedures you can follow as well as collection call procedures and examples of conversations you might have. Credit card procedures for automatic charge accounts, information on COD payments received from shippers, what to do with all the small balance accounts you may have, what to do when you get an NSF check, Dunning letters procedures and examples of many letters you might be able to use. Information on payment plans, placing accounts with a collection agency and how to place them. How to write off bad debt, what you need to have on your credit applications, and examples of credit applications.

Also included are Federal credit laws you must follow. Information on doing business online, electronic contracts and electronic signatures. I have also included information on state laws regarding adding interest and/or late fees.

After working in all facets of credit and collections, Michelle Dunn knows the credit business from the practical side. She begins by telling how important it is to establish credit policies, and then she shows us how to do it. There are sample credit applications, information on collecting credit ratings online, guidelines for handling private information, plus forms and sample letters covering every step of the collection process, from friendly reminders all the way to legal proceedings. She even includes scripts for various types of telephone calls.

Many businesses do not have a credit and collections policy. The reasons for this could be that the business owner is afraid that asking for the money that is owed to them will make their customer mad and he will go somewhere else with his business. If they are not paying you, is this a bad thing? Why waste your time chasing money when you can have good paying customers. There will always be a few customers who are payment problems but the fewer the better and you have some control over that.

Also, many business owners do not know how to get the customer to pay or don't know what they can legally do to obtain payment. This book will help you get paid on time and therefore save you money and help you to make more money.

The longer you don't do anything about getting paid, the chances you will get paid are much less. This book is to help you, the business owner to keep your customers, and get paid. Having a credit and collections policy sets a positive credit tone for your business. It also lets potential customers know that you mean business! Don't let your slow paying customers control you, it's up to you to take the wheel and drive.

Some FAQ's that are covered in chapters of the book:

How common is it that there are consistently problems collecting money from customers? **Some business owners, especially new business owners are so eager for a sale that they don't document or discuss payment, then they don't want to offend the customer by asking for their money.**

Is it worth it for a small business to attempt to go after the money due to them? **It depends on the amount of the bill and what information you already have on the customer. Such as contact information so you can get a hold of them or even take them to small claims court.**

What legal issues are involved with collecting your money? **You will have to follow the FDCPA, Fair Debt Collection Practices Act and any laws in your state. Also you should also have a contract or signed agreement to protect yourself.**

What are some of the ways a company can protect themselves or precautions they can make? Should they change the way they do business in any way? **Always get a credit application and check references if extending credit. Have a good credit policy and stick to it!**

What are the steps that a company needs to take to collect money due to them? **If your calls or letters don't prompt payment, you can sue them in small claims court or place them for collection.**

Get your Clients to make you more money!

Do you give your clients thank you gifts at the holidays or any other time to thank them for their business? Calendars, mugs, mouse pads? Give them the gift the helps them and helps you!

If you educate your clients on an effective credit policy, your job just became easier. You will get accounts sooner; you will have credit applications and other helpful documentation when you need it. So help your clients help you and collect more money.

Order today! www.michelledunn.com

HOW TO HELP YOU GET PAID

From the Author

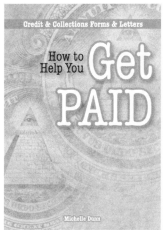

I created this book because so many clients and other entrepreneurs who own their own businesses ask me for examples of collection letters. I thought it would be beneficial for everyone if I compiled several examples into an easy-to-use reference. This will allow everyone, including YOU, to possess different collection letters to utilize for different situations as they arise.

The letters can be changed to suit your business or situation, and/or they can be used as is.

This book includes the following types of letters and forms:
- Before Court Action
- Check Returned
- Credit Reporting
- Deductions
- Envelope Enclosed
- Legal Action
- NSF checks
- Partial Payments
- Payment Obligations
- Payment Reminder
- Placing for collection
- Request for Payment Letter
- Return Call Letter
- Small Amounts
- The 3-Letter Series
- We Value Fairness

Bonus Items:
Credit Application
Request a Letter

HOW TO GET YOUR CUSTOMERS TO PAY

From the Author

ISBN# 0-9706645-2-4

Why not have more money? Wouldn't you rather spend your time doing what you enjoy?

Writing a clear concise letter that generates a result is an art. When you buy *Fast, Easy, Effective Letters, How to Get Your Customers to Pay,* you will learn how to create and use letters to collect more money with less effort.

Your letter should: Tell the reason for your letter in the first sentence; Explain more about the first sentence in your second sentence; Suggest a solution; and, thank the recipient.

You can use the letters and forms in this book to collect the money that is owed to you. If you use these ready to use letters and forms in this book as part of your credit policy you will:

- Have more money
- Have and keep good customers that pay with minimum effort on your part
- Be successful

A few Tips Michelle shares with you in her book are:
1. Send a reminder immediately when account is past due
2. Tell your reason for the letter in the first sentence
3. Include the balance due amount
4. Make collection letters short and to the point
5. Offer a solution
6. Enclose an envelope for payment
7. Be firm
8. Assume the debtor will pay
9. Be friendly
10. Make each letter stronger

Order your copy today, read the rest of the tips and collect more money today!

BOOK ORDER FORM

Online orders: www.michelledunn.com
> Securely accepting Visa, MasterCard, Discover, Paypal, checks, Debit & Credit cards

Email orders: michelle@michelledunn.com

Postal orders: Mail to: Never Dunn Publishing LLC, Michelle Dunn, PO Box 40, Plymouth, NH 03264 USA.

Please send the following books:

❑ *How to Make Money Collecting Money, Starting a Collection Agency, 3rd Edition*   ISBN# is 0-9706645-6-7
$62.95, E-Book $57.95

❑ *Become the Squeaky Wheel, A Credit and Collections Guide for Everyone*
ISBN#: 0-9706645-1-6
$34.99, E-Book $29.99

❑ *How to Help You Get Paid, Credit & Collections Forms & Letters*
$14.95; E-Book $9.95

❑ *The First Book of Effective Collection Agency Letters & Forms*
ISBN#: 0970664540
E-Book $19.95

❑ *How to Get Your Customers to Pay, Fast, Easy, Effective Letters*
ISBN#: 0970664524
E-Book $19.95

Shipping: **INCLUDED** in all prices above (to U.S. Addresses)

Payment: ❑ Check
(enclose with form, payable to "Michelle Dunn Writer, LLC")

❑ Credit or Debit   ❑ Visa   ❑ MasterCard   ❑ Discover

Card#: _____

Name on Card: _____Exp. Date: ____/____

Shipping Address: _____

_____

For more information on any of Michelle Dunn's other books
please visit *www.michelledunn.com*
or email at michelle@michelledunn.com

Thank you for your order!

AN INVALUABLE RESOURCE

DO PEOPLE OWE YOU MONEY?
DO YOU WANT TO GET PAID?

Join Credit & Collections today for free networking, e-books, tips, forms and letters to help you collect the money owed to you. Visit www.credit-and-collections.com today and join thousands of professionals who work together and support each other in the debt collection industry.

Also visit the website often for updates and special discount offers available to members only.

BONUS ITEM

STARTING A COLLECTION AGENCY CHECKLIST

Use this page as a worksheet as you start your own debt collection agency. Before you quit your "day" job you can take these steps to be prepared when you open your agency.

- ❑ 1. Research collection agencies online and in your area. See what services they offer and what they charge.
- ❑ 2. Start buying office supplies and setting up your office.
- ❑ 3. Come up with a company name and register that name with your state.
- ❑ 4. Once you have a name, open a bank account and PO Box.
- ❑ 5. Create letterhead, business cards, promotional materials and a tag line.
- ❑ 6. Write a business plan.
- ❑ 7. Write a marketing plan.
- ❑ 8. Join credit & debt collection associations to see what they offer and how you can learn more about the industry.
- ❑ 9. Join local associations such as the Chamber of Commerce or a Rotary club.
- ❑ 10. Research skip tracing options.
- ❑ 11. Research bonding, licensing and insurance.
- ❑ 12. Research or create a website.
- ❑ 13. Read magazines and books regarding debt collection and credit policies.
- ❑ 14. Apply for a Federal Employer Identification number using form S4 at www.irs.gov/pub
- ❑ 15. Research debt collection software.
- ❑ 16. Create a list of potential clients.
- ❑ 17. Email me with any questions at michelle@michelledunn.com

NOTES